UNTAMED

A TESTIMONY OF OVERCOMING THE ODDS

LAWRENCE BUTLER

Published by: HigherLife Publishing and Marketing
PO Box 623307
Oviedo, FL 32762
(407) 563-4806
HigherLifePublishing.com

ISBN: 978-1-958211-99-1 paperback
ISBN: 978-1-958211-96-0 ebook
Library of Congress 1-12346019251

Printed in the United States of America
10 9 8 7 6 5 4 3 2 1

Dedication

This book is dedicated to two people
who made me and this book possible:

Bobbie Jarrett

Coach Charles Leggett

Contents

Foreword

The first time we met Lawrence Butler, we could sense his unwavering strength and compassion.

As we got to know him better, we learned that he had endured more hardship than anyone we had ever met. We first came in contact with Lawrence when he rented our venue for his company's Christmas holiday party years ago, and even then, his generosity, compassion, and profound insight into human nature were apparent to us. Years later, my husband and I battled the fallout from radiation and cancer treatments. Despite Lawrence's busy schedule, he went out of his way to drive us to out-of-town doctors' appointments and ensured we were comfortable during our trips.

We are not the only ones Lawrence seeks to help. He genuinely cares about people in the community and is a humble person with grand ideas and a big heart. When he began writing his book, we stood by him, unaware of the trials and tribulations he had faced in his life: brushes with death, humiliation, cruelty, disrespect, and racial prejudice. We knew him as a man of God, an entrepreneur, an athlete, a philosopher, and a philanthropist, as well as a loving husband, father, and friend. Until he shared the draft pages with us during his writing process, we had no idea of his challenges—beginning with his difficult birth.

Despite facing numerous tragedies and seemingly insurmountable challenges throughout his life, Lawrence found the strength to persevere and rise above them, inspiring others with his determination. His book beautifully demonstrates how he has lead his life and business with love, compassion, and unwavering courage rather than allowing fear to dictate his actions. It is his testament to the resilience of the human spirit.

Lawrence's life has been filled with violence and hate, but he chooses to focus on learning lessons from those who sought to harm him as he lovingly acknowledges caring individuals who helped him grow and succeed. Observing Lawrence as he continues to make a positive difference in the world is uplifting and inspiring.

Pem Pfisterer Clark
Nationally Syndicated Radio Show Host,
"Wedding Planning With Pem"
Author, *For Better or For Worse, Just Shoot Me Now*

Glenn L. Johnson
Businessman/Retailer
Former Mayor, Henderson, Kentucky

Preface

My name is Lawrence Butler. I am known as one of the few successful African American business owners in welding and plumbing in my hometown of Henderson, Kentucky. Although today I am viewed as a success, I had a humble beginning. Without a doubt, life was hard. But those difficulties became invaluable resources in the form of lessons I learned along the way.

I entered the world in Indianapolis, Indiana, in November 1955. I was the firstborn of my mother and father, neither of whom raised me. Instead, at just six weeks old, my mother took me to West Tennessee to live with my grandparents, paying them $50 monthly for my keep. I've been told that I was not a healthy baby. I suffered from a heart murmur, which put physical limits on what I could do as a child.

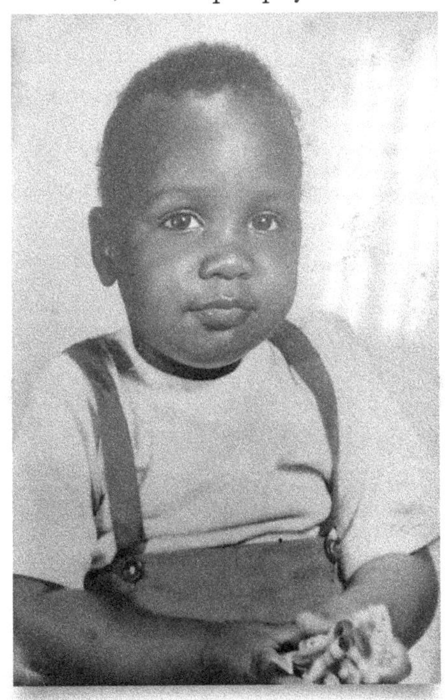

Lawrence Butler

My grandparents raised me when no one else would. For that, I am grateful. A hardworking couple, their livelihood came from sharecropping. We lived in a small, wooden house with no running water and only four rooms. Inside those rooms, 13 people shared space—my grandparents, eight of their 13 children, and three grandchildren.

The older boys had a regular-size bed, but we smaller boys slept in a half-size bed or on the floor if there was company. When I think about it, we always had company—whether humans

My grandparents

or the rats that chewed their way through the walls of our dwelling. I would go so far as to say that the rats lived better than we did because they ate what we ate and, at night, tried to feed on us. My grandmother lit candles to keep the rats away from us. But once the candles burned out, it was on! We would wake up screaming from the rats biting us.

We always had plenty to eat and plenty of work. I started helping my grandmother in the cotton field at five or six. We picked cotton, placed it in our smaller bags, and then emptied those into my grandmother's sack. Two of us worked on a row. If we fell behind, my grandmother caught us up. We got paid the same as grownups.

There were other jobs, too. We had chickens that we'd order through the mail. We could get 50 to 100 baby chicks for about $1.

My grandparents' house where I grew up

We had cows for milk, raised hogs for meat, and picked fruits such as plums, apples, peaches, or whatever was in season.

Nothing was wasted. I remember when my grandmother hung hog meat to cure; the rats ate most of it. What was left would sometimes rot, but grandmother boiled "the skippers out," and we'd eat it. Later, I learned that maggots had infested the meat, and the adults called them "skippers" to get us to eat.

Most can't imagine living like this. I didn't know that people lived any other way. But we were healthy, and most importantly, we were taught about God.

God and the Greyhound

In the 1960s and 1970s, Tennessee was a very different place. With more African Americans demanding their basic rights as American-born citizens, the country once again found itself in the middle of a civil war. Many became casualties in the struggle between the old ways and the *right* way. And I was almost one of them.

The year I was born, the United States Supreme Court took its first step toward a blended society by ordering schools to desegregate. However, it appeared Tennessee didn't get the memo because it wasn't until I entered high school that I attended classes with White students. The association between Whites and Blacks, according to unwritten but fiercely enforced laws, ended there—or was supposed to. We were not to interact with White children or young people. To defy these social stipulations usually resulted in death for the African American. More than 40 years after high school, I still remember the fear and hurt generated by the deaths of young African American men and the maiming of young White women rumored to be in romantic relationships.

The dangers were real and finally landed at my front door.

At age 17, I graduated from high school and was employed at the Winter Garden, a plant in Bells, Tennessee. This company is where food was prepared for packaging and then shipped to grocery stores nationwide.

One afternoon, I had just left my grandparents' house and was riding my bicycle to a friend's when a young white woman stopped me. She asked about my uncle, who was also 17. Later, I learned they were romantically involved and often met in the woods.

My verbal interaction with her was brief, and I didn't think anything more about it. But our innocent exchange had been seen, and to some, the rules had been broken.

I never made it to my friend's house. I went back home, and roughly 45 minutes later, an African American gentleman, a sharecropper on the land owned by the young woman's father, came to speak with my grandfather. He had witnessed the young woman and me speaking and came to warn us that the girl's father had heard about the inadvertent meeting in front of my grandparent's house.

My uncle and I chose to leave our hometown immediately. He decided to move to Louisville. Less than 12 hours after we received the warning, I was on a Greyhound bus headed to Evansville, Indiana, where another of my uncles lived. I was relieved when the doors finally closed on the bus, and it pulled out of the bus station at Humboldt, Tennessee.

It wasn't until then that I felt safe.

My grandparents' house when I left home

On My Way

It was a 12-hour trip from home to Evansville. I sat in my seat, somewhat stunned at my life's sudden turn. My question, "How did I get here?" took me to a place of reflection I wasn't sure I was ready to visit—but I went anyway. Looking back at my life, I had to acknowledge that I was born into a state of rejection. For reasons I still don't understand, I personified the anger and disappointment my grandparents felt toward my mother and that my mother felt toward herself.

I put a face to it: my grandfather disliked my mother, and my mother disliked her father. He did things to *me* to get to her. For example, he would say things like, "The buzzard laid him in the sun and hatched him" about me. When my mother visited, she made sure to treat me in such a way so that I would never want to leave home and, therefore, was the favorite recipient of the turbulent emotions that swelled within it. It is said that children are like sponges—that they soak in everything around them. It's true. I was a sponge that soaked in their snide remarks, their unkind gestures, and the humiliation of my mother's choices, of which I was a direct result. I was not very old when I began comprehending the emotional distance between myself and my mother. One day, I watched a dog chase someone away from her pups to protect them. I thought, *A dog thinks more about her young than my mother thinks of me.*

That's when things started to change, and I grew angry. Thankfully, God gave me something to nurture my broken spirit, something I could dedicate myself to and from which I could reap some positive, emotional rewards. I was four or maybe five years old the first time I saw the Harlem Globetrotters. They inspired me. After seeing the

Globetrotters, I decided to pick up a basketball. It was there that I found my peace.

You see, basketball was something I could do and do alone. And with the way my family, especially my mother, directed their dysfunction toward me, I knew that alone was a good place to be. So yes, basketball was my peace. It was also one of the ways God used to heal, teach, and show me that He loved me. I will say, though, that sometimes, when God moves, it doesn't feel like love. It hurts much like ripping a scab from a wound. I remember one of those times distinctly. During my eighth-grade year, my basketball coach was Coach Fair. I didn't think he lived up to his name. In fact, from my 12-year-old perspective, I believed wholeheartedly that he singled me out and even picked on me.

Looking back, it's true that Coach Fair was hard on me, but not out of meanness. I believe he demanded a higher performance because he saw something in me—something I couldn't see in myself—talent, ability, value. I truly thought I was giving him my best, but my best wasn't good enough for him. I believed that *I* wasn't good enough. The more he pushed, the harder I tried. The harder I tried, the more I failed … or so I thought.

Finally, it all came to a head. One day during basketball practice, out of sheer frustration, Coach Fair benched me and chose my *younger* cousin to play my position. I was

Coach Fair

humiliated. Most teenage boys would never admit to crying, and I was no different. So that day, while my younger cousin played my position during that practice, I sat on the bench. My eyes started to water. Coach Fair saw the heartbreak I couldn't keep from running down my face. He pulled me off the bench and put me back into the game. I tried so hard, but I kept messing up! I couldn't do anything right.

Coach Fair did it again—he pulled me out of the game, but this time he played the position himself. The next chance I got to play, I mirrored his movements. He went through the plays a second time. Again, I copied him. I learned to do what he asked of me the minute he showed me what he wanted. It was a moment of illumination for both of us. Coach Fair learned to teach his players by example, and I learned I could do anything.

That day, which started out as humiliating and devastating, turned out to be pivotal in terms of my emotional and spiritual growth. That day, which initially felt like my lifeline was being yanked out of my hands, brought a depth of healing that continues even now. Why?

Through Coach Fair's persistence, he showed me that I was the only one putting limits on myself. When he was thrust into changing times, my coach embraced a humble spirit, accepting that he, too, had to change if he was going to shape us into a winning team. Coach Fair's courage to change prompted me to embrace change as well. I began to believe that while some might expect me to fail, even tell me that I would, their opinion didn't define me. Their words couldn't prevent my success. Only my choices could. Thanks to Coach Fair, I released my grip on my low expectations of myself and started reaching higher.

My mother

My father

City Life

My thoughts were deep as I traveled the 12 hours from Tennessee to my new home in Evansville. Let's face it: running for your life can put you in a reflective state.

As I neared the big city, I reminded myself there was a gap between wanting and laziness. To achieve something or not could be defined by how much I wanted it and how hard I was willing to work for it.

I admit that I was also apprehensive about this move. I realized I wouldn't have family or friends with whom to play basketball. While I was excited to be heading to a new life, it was also frightening to not have the comfort of anyone or anything familiar nearby.

My first day in Evansville didn't do much to relieve my anxiety. My introduction to the city was witnessing a young man snatch a lady's purse. I had never seen this before, and my instinct was to try to help. I chased the thief but didn't catch him. I was sorry then, but now I believe this could have been a blessing. People settled things differently in the city, arming themselves with knives and guns. In the country, we used sticks and fists. All of these can be deadly, of course, but some of those weapons are more so than others.

On my second day in Evansville, I found a basketball game. I was ecstatic. I quickly discovered that streetball and high school basketball are two different animals. High school basketball has a team, referees, coaches, and cheerleaders. Streetball comes with an unwritten code—bring it or stay home. Anything else, anything in between, can get you hurt.

Unfortunately, I learned that the hard way.

That first basketball game in the city is one I will never forget. I was an unknown commodity to this group, which automatically put me in a class of those to be distrusted and disliked. I understand this now. My 17-year-old self didn't have a clue. I was so thrilled to be back in the game that I loved so much that, at first, I didn't understand that this wasn't the same. Where I was used to playing team ball, this was every man for himself. I adapted and quickly morphed into this type of player, using moves my opponent couldn't defend. I was new. This was his turf. And there was one way this was going to end—abruptly.

He punched me. Hard. Right in the face. I was shocked but not stupid. I left the game. I wasn't afraid to fight, but I was outnumbered. So, I exited the game and headed home. I still don't know why, but I made an unplanned detour to the home of my uncle's girlfriend. She and a friend were there. After hearing my story, her friend asked me if I still wanted to play ball. I assured him that I did. He stood up, grabbed his gun, stuck it in his pants, and said, "Let's go."

We walked back to the game. It goes without saying that I got to play. From that day on, there was no resistance to my presence on the court. Why? It goes back to a basic and unfortunate principle that spans all races and socioeconomic classes. It's found in the boardroom, the classroom, and on the street—it's about who you know.

They knew him; he knew me; and that association gave me credibility. Those hostile basketball players adjusted their attitudes because he had my back.

After that, I played with them every chance I got. When I wasn't working, I was playing. It was truly the most fun I ever had playing basketball. I started building a reputation as an athlete. People started recognizing me, and I began realizing that I was a good player on my own merit and not because of my association with a team. I started walking a little taller. I began feeling more at home.

My good fortune continued as I made my first real friend in Evansville. His name was Kevin.

Kevin

Friendship is an invaluable resource in anyone's life. It's especially important to a 17-year-old kid who left home under the threat of death and arrived in a new city, only to be punched in the face during a basketball game.

It was at a basketball game that I met Kevin and at a basketball game that I lost to him. We all lost to him.

Kevin was also 17 and loved basketball as much as I did. It's been almost 50 years, and I can still see his face. He was very quiet and reserved. Kevin reminded me a lot of myself, but, while I was starting to break the chains of feeling worthless and expendable, he was still shackled by them.

Kevin was in the crowd one day watching me play basketball, and after the game, we started talking.

From that moment on, we were friends. Every day, we'd play basketball—*every* day.

Kevin and I were friends for two weeks, a lifetime at 17. That's why what happened next hurt as much as if we'd been friends for years.

I remember the day clearly. Kevin and I were playing basketball with some girls in an alley. The alley was near a park around Blackford and U.S. 41-South. We were hanging out, talking, and having fun. In the middle of our game, Kevin's brother and his brother's friend drove up. Kevin's brother asked us if we wanted to smoke marijuana. I didn't. I always believed my parents didn't want me because I'd done something wrong. Therefore, I always tried not to do anything else wrong. Taking illegal drugs is wrong. I told Kevin's brother that I didn't smoke and went back to playing basketball. Kevin got in the car and smoked with his brother. When the game was over, I went back to the car and told Kevin I was leaving. I asked him to come, but he wouldn't leave. He said he would head to my house once he was finished smoking.

Time and distance are both relative depending on the circumstances surrounding them. Yes, both are used as a point of measure, but how fast or slow time goes depends on whether you enjoy what you're doing. Distance can be short or long depending on the obstacles in your path or if your shoes pinch.

I lived about three blocks from where we'd been playing basketball. Not far, all things considered. But on this day, it was far enough.

I'd left the alley and Kevin just minutes before, but those minutes were long enough to save my life. I wasn't there when two White men decided to murder my best friend. As the story goes, the two men set out in their truck, looking for a Black man to shoot. That's when they found Kevin. They shot him in the chest with a shotgun.

I didn't know all this when I heard the ambulance race past my house. After all, I'd just gotten home, and the keening sound of the ambulance siren wasn't uncommon. It was city noise. Then the phone started ringing. A friend called to check on me. He'd heard that a young Black man had been killed in the Blackford area where I was known to play basketball, and he thought it was me. I couldn't move fast enough. I hung up the phone and ran the three blocks back to the alley. When I got there, a crowd had formed. There was blood on the street. Kevin's blood—it was all that was left of him.

His body had already been removed.

I'm not sure what else I can say about this. It's hard to describe violence and the lingering pall it leaves on a person's soul. I can say that I started to question whether I should stay in Evansville. The problem was that I didn't have any place else to go. If I went home, I'd be killed. That was unquestionable. If I stayed, I might end up like Kevin. Then again, there was a chance that I would be fine. When there's a choice between a certain death or a chance at life, it's pretty clear what most will choose. I stayed. I was afraid, but I stayed.

I'm glad I did. Once again, God moved His hand, and I was given the opportunity to turn my grief into positive action.

The violence and shock of Kevin's death hit me with the emotional force of an 18-wheeler colliding at full speed into a crash dummy. On the outside, my 17-year-old self was strong with youth and vitality. On the inside, my heart and soul had aged and cracked like brittle bones. The Bible promises that out of what Satan means for evil, God brings forth something good. At the time, I couldn't see His hand. But 40 years later, I know that's what God did for me. He didn't let the evil that murdered Kevin go unabated. How? He once again put me in a situation that came down to a choice. With this, He breathed life back into my soul.

While I would have loved to focus solely on basketball, a man has to work if he wants to eat. One of the first things I did as a resident of Evansville was to look for a job. I landed one at Red Lobster. That's where I met Ti.

Ti was Vietnamese, about my age, and became my second friend.

One night, not long after Kevin's death, Ti and I were working at the restaurant as busboys.

Have you ever noticed that with God, there are no coincidences? That He leaves nothing to chance? He is always there, inviting us to be part of His plans. He doesn't force us. He guides. He whispers. He urges.

That's where we humans usually drop the ball—we fail to listen, and then we fail to act.

That night, I wasn't thinking about any of this. I just knew that I needed to get my dirty dishes where they could be washed for use by the next hungry patrons. I walked in to deliver my load and found Ti backed against the wall by three White men, also busboys. They were spouting their poison at him, saying that they were going to "whip him up." I had a split second to embrace God's timing or run away, leaving Ti to his fate. I chose to stand with Ti. I joined him on the wall and said, "Whip us both."

Prejudice is the type of evil that prefers to operate in numbers. Two on three has better odds than three on one, so they slunk away and left us alone.

I have never regretted joining Ti on that wall. I know what it's like to be alone, and I didn't want to leave Ti in that predicament. From that day on, we were friends. I still missed my basketball buddy Kevin, but God gave me a new friend, and I was grateful. Ti's stay in the U.S. was brief. After graduating from college, he returned to Vietnam with the aspiration of becoming a doctor. Maybe somewhere in that part of the world, Ti is doing what he set out to do. And maybe, just maybe, he's once again standing at a wall, helping people fight battles with illness and disease so they won't have to be alone.

Coach Leggett

SOMETHING HAPPENS WHEN YOU STAND BETWEEN A ROCK AND A HARD PLACE—YOU HAVE TO GO DEEP FOR THE STRENGTH AND ENDURANCE TO STAY THERE. Strength is born in adversity and past experiences. Ti and I were in just such a spot that night at Red Lobster. When we came through unscathed and fast friends, I couldn't tell you what he thought about or what he reflected upon. I can only tell you about myself.

Believe it or not, I thought about a White man named Charles Leggett. During my high school basketball days, I called him Coach, along with some other names. Thoughts of Coach Leggett naturally gave way to thoughts of *team* and the potential, the power that comes from the joining of a common purpose and passion.

With such introspection, I became 15 again. I was leaving an all-Black high school—thanks to desegregation—and doing my best to integrate into a sea of White teenagers, some of whom didn't want me there. For sure, some of their parents didn't want me there. But one person did. Coach Leggett.

I didn't know this until I was a grown man with children. To be fair, though, I will say that even as a teenager, I could tell he was willing to give

Coach Leggett with Lawrence

Black athletes a shot. On the first day of basketball practice, I didn't watch my competition. I watched him. Remember, I was an unwanted child being raised by my grandparents. By this time, I'd gotten pretty good at reading people—a safeguard in warding off emotional blows.

As I watched Coach trying to get a bead on the White players, I saw his face change. Whenever a Black athlete made a layup or scored some points, he had a smirk that hinted at favor. Now, I was the smallest player in the gym. I was only about five feet and two inches tall and 105 pounds with rocks in my pocket, but I really wanted to play basketball. I went through all of the drills except for the scrimmage. Coach wouldn't let me scrimmage. I thought he was trying to get rid of me. He succeeded. I walked out that day and didn't look back ... for a while, anyway.

I spent my sophomore year on the outside looking in. Basketball had been my anchor, and I'd lost it. It was odd, though, to hear how much Coach Leggett appeared to favor Black players. At least, that was the talk from team members. I was dumbfounded. He didn't favor me, and I was better than the White players he put in. Heck, I was better than a lot of the Black players, too. The only thing that they had going for them was height.

His team—Blacks and Whites—loved him. To me, he sucked. Looking back, I can see now that what Coach Leggett did for Black athletes was monumental. Think about it—in the first year of an integrated high school, he welcomed Black players on his team. He even played them on the first string. It couldn't have made him popular among Whites, but he did it anyway. He raised the bar for Blacks, and they respected him for it. He also had a knack for turning people who seemingly had nothing in common into a team.

Under his guidance, Black and White teens became teammates and then friends. The more I watched the evolution, the more I wanted to be part of it. I longed to prove myself and despaired that the day would never come.

Eventually, it did.

Coach Leggett was very good at mining the student landscape—Black or White—for talent. He'd hold games of 21 or coordinate basketball tournaments between the freshmen, sophomore, junior, and senior classes. Only in *these* games were basketball players banned from participating.

During this intra-class tournament, popular opinion favored the senior class as the winner. The juniors were next, followed by the sophomores. My class upset the bracket. With me leading them, the sophomores beat the seniors and juniors, and Coach Leggett watched. I have to say, winning felt good. Doing it in front of Coach Leggett, well, that felt great. That victory was the impetus I needed to try out for the basketball team again.

Principal Lanthem of my high school

It Still Wasn't Happening

My junior year began with a great deal of anticipation on my part. Imagine how you'd feel if you'd been lost in the desert, barely surviving on drops of water here and there. Then suddenly, before your eyes, you see a pool of water. That deep, do-it-or-die longing for a real drink of water was much like my emotional desire to play basketball with a team again. My longing wasn't just for the game. It was, in part, a need for approval from a coach who hadn't given it so far. Yes, I wanted to play basketball, but I desperately wanted him to show everyone he'd chosen me, that he approved of me. That I belonged. I believed that this was the year that it would happen.

I couldn't have been more wrong.

Life seldom happens the way you imagine it will. Yes, I tried out for and made the team. But I rarely got the chance to play. Game after game, I spent much of my time on the bench while aching to hold that basketball in my hands.

Soon, I noticed a pattern emerging. If, and only if, my team was behind would Coach Leggett put me in.

When we were trailing, Coach would let me on the court long enough for me to get the team caught up. Then he'd pull me out, and I'd sit on the bench the rest of the game. The gym would be rocking. The crowd would be calling for me, chanting my name. But the noise, the rumble, all fell on deaf ears because Coach Leggett didn't acknowledge the fans or me.

That's how things went the entire season.

Finally, the tournament rolled around. I remember one tournament game. I was put in to guard Isaiah Wade. I'm positive you don't recognize that name. I'll never forget it. He was five feet, eight inches tall, and the second-leading scorer in Tennessee. I was five feet, two inches tall, 105 pounds, and, at the moment, playing for a team that was in a tug-of-war match for the lead.

During the second quarter, Coach Leggett thrust me into this real-life David and Goliath scenario. Isaiah Wade was a good athlete and one whom I admired. Since it was my job to be in his space, I watched him, read him, and learned his strategies. This is a good lesson in life. Anytime you are put in a situation that seems bigger than you, remember:

1. Don't panic.
2. Shut your mouth.
3. Watch and learn.

By doing these things, I learned how to play defense against him. I'm sure that I frustrated him. Every move he made, I was there. He scored only four points while I guarded him. I begrudged him those points, but just a little bit. After all, my team pulled ahead and won the game. I was ecstatic!

A hard-fought victory didn't alter Coach Leggett's practice schedule. The next day found our team back out on the court, running drills and practicing plays. It was pretty routine. What made that day extraordinary was what happened next.

The route home took me past a small grocery store owned by a White man. After practice, I walked home and, naturally, passed that business. When the White owner saw me, he came outside and said, "Butler, you played a basketball game." Then he gave me snacks and a drink from his store. I felt like a king!

That feeling was short-lived.

It was time for the second game of the tournament.

Almost from tip-off, my team started losing ground. Soon, we weren't just behind; we were being annihilated. If we lost, the tournament was over for us. The desperation in the air was thick. Our fans shouted my name, calling for Coach Leggett to put me in. The gym rocked with it. Their chants fell on deaf ears—at least for most of the game.

Then, with 45 seconds left, he put me in. The best that I recall, we were down by 15 or 20 points.

There was no coming back from that in less than a minute. I knew that before I even got off the bench.

But I went through the motions. I stood up, walked over to check in my number, and went onto the basketball court. The referee blew the whistle, and the game resumed. The basketball hit the ground with a *thud, thud, thud*. The rubber of the players' tennis shoes squeaked against the surface of the gym floor. Plays were being called, and the fans and cheerleaders produced their own ear-splitting cacophony.

There was plenty of movement, plenty of action occurring on the basketball court. And none of it was coming from me. I stood there as still as a statue with my arms folded across my chest and tears streaming down my face. I didn't move. Not once. The clock ran down, the buzzer sounded, and it was over. We'd lost. Bad.

With the game concluded, I walked off the court and into the locker room to change clothes. I got back on the bus with the rest of the team, and we went home.

That was a dark day. I hated Coach Leggett. I hated him with every fiber of my being. He wouldn't let me play. He'd rather lose a game than let me play. Not Blacks. *Me*. I'd spent the last 45 seconds of my cherished basketball season poised in a gesture of defeated defiance. I was heartbroken. I was enraged.

I was ready to shake his eyeballs out of his head. But I wasn't done.

You see, some of my angst wasn't at Coach Leggett. It was at me. I was ashamed. I've always been proud, but I knew deep down that some of my teammates were better than me. At the same time, I'd felt ready for that game. Yet, he wouldn't let me play until the score was too far gone, and it no longer mattered whether I was on the court or not. It was humiliating.

I felt a lot of things. The one emotion I didn't embrace—surrender. I didn't wallow. I looked forward. In so doing, I asked my grandmother for leg weights. I wanted strength in my legs so that I could dunk. She told me what I already knew. If I wanted weights, working for them was the only way to get them. That's what I did. I spent several weeks working in the fields, earning money: I picked cotton, pulled up cotton plants, and dug out stumps. Finally, I had the money. Not long after, I had the five-pound weights. I wore them everywhere. I wore them to the plant where I'd landed a job; I wore them in the tub. I'd wear them while I practiced basketball. I wore them and dreamt of two things—squaring off with my nemesis, Coach Leggett, and getting a girlfriend.

Putting Coach in his place was where most of my energy surged. I practiced basketball and pictured his face on the rim of the hoop. I'd try to knock his face off that rim and into the net. When I dribbled, I imagined pounding his face with the ball. I practiced by visualizing that I was playing against myself. Truthfully, I was trying to beat him. All my focus that summer was on basketball. I could play every part of the game. I could rebound, play defense, and make layups. I breathed, ate, and slept basketball. Heck, I wore 10-pound weights around my legs throughout that hot season. And since my mind was so absorbed in perfecting the game, my body decided to get on board. I grew four inches that summer. I went back to school a giant. The day Coach Leggett saw me, my new size, and the way I was playing—he just smiled. Needless to say, my senior year got off to a smug start.

Simultaneously, I felt like many seniors feel. It was the last year of high school, and I wanted to make my mark. Yet, I refused to try out for the basketball team. My body had changed. My skill set had changed. Coach Leggett knew it. And I knew he knew it. But I was not going to play for him unless he begged. I wanted him to beg me to play for him the way I'd begged him to let me play. (Yes, even teenage boys can be dramatic.)

Then, one day, I was in class when a note was sent to me from Coach. He asked me to play for him. Coach Leggett didn't exactly beg, but my 17-year-old mind interpreted it that way. Still, I wouldn't play. I stood my ground just like in that last horrible basketball game.

Coach Leggett took another approach. He told my uncle, who is the same age as me, that he'd start me. I didn't budge. Then, I received a piece of information that tipped the scales decidedly in Coach Leggett's favor. I found out I'd get to ride the bus with the cheerleaders and girls' basketball team. That's when I agreed to play. You have to remember that I lived out in the country. The best-looking thing we ever saw was a newborn calf.

Once I agreed to play, I was his guy. I still didn't like him, but he let me play. He even told the other players, "Give the ball to Lawrence, and everybody go down court. He'll get it there." Getting to play and those few moments of veneration brought us a gossamer-thin thread of peace. Oh, and in case you're wondering, my senior year saw yet another of my heart's desires fulfilled—I got a girlfriend!

30th Class Reunion

50th Class Reunion

After Leggett

Once I left high school, I didn't expect to look back and reflect on Coach Leggett as a force of positive change in my life. Quite frankly, I didn't plan to think about him at all. I was wrong. After Kevin's murder, I needed an emotional outlet. Naturally, I turned to basketball. I heard about basketball games held at Evansville's C K Newsome Community Center. I also heard that college players would showcase their skills there. It had been a while since I was tested in the basketball realm, and I needed the challenge. I needed a goal to absorb my thoughts and exhaust my turbulent emotions. I decided to check out the games. The year was 1973.

During one of my first visits to the community center, I was picked to play ball with the college guys. I was exhilarated. The more I played, however, the more my exhilaration diminished. I was a good basketball player. These guys were great and played above my skill level. The bar had been raised—again. As the pressure mounted, an old determination reawakened within me. In high school, like with Coach Leggett, I had two choices: quit or step up. If life had taught me anything, it was never to fear a challenge.

My nearly two decades on this planet had also taught me to be honest. I was honest enough with myself to know that my physical fitness needed a boost. I started jumping rope—a habit that I've fostered to this day. Slowly, my body strengthened, as did my mental acuity. Remember, I watch and learn. I immersed myself in learning from these incredible athletes. I was young, single, and able to direct my focus on this sport. I still worked at Red Lobster, lived with my uncle, and spent every spare minute playing ball at the community center. Time continued to pass, and the world entered the year 1974. I was 18.

One day, a woman approached me during my visit to the center. She said she'd been watching me play and asked if I'd be interested in playing college ball. She told me that she'd spoken with the basketball coach at the University of Evansville, and he said I could try out as a walk-on. She emphasized there were no guarantees.

Here's the thing: I hated school until my senior year. I didn't want to study and knew deep down that I wasn't a pro ball player. I would never make it to the NBA, so college ball had no appeal for me. I respectfully declined. Something that even my high school coach didn't know was that my knees were hurting; I didn't understand that my quick physical growth was causing my pain. Even during games in my senior year, no one knew I would cry after games because my knees hurt so bad. That situation made my decision not to play college ball at Evansville that year—the same year that the entire team was killed in a plane crash.

I kept playing ball at the C K Newsome Center, but my life started evolving outside of that. At that point, I began to wonder if basketball was for me. People often fail to understand the emptiness a child with no mother or father carries in their heart. Basketball, for some, is just a game, a job, a means in or out of the hood, or a way to steer clear of trouble. The ball serves various purposes for different people—a surrogate for their parents, perhaps. For me, it was both. However, after the University of Evansville plane crash, I felt the need for a new adventure; basketball wasn't doing it for me anymore. It was a tough decision; it reminded me of not making the team my sophomore year and how it felt like I'd let down my parents. My decision not to play at Evansville was like my sophomore defeat all over again.

In addition to this, in April of 1976, my first daughter was born. With her birth, I officially moved into the category of no longer being my only responsibility. I looked at this tiny creature and wanted her to have what I didn't—a father. I needed to provide for her physical, spiritual, and emotional needs. I was working full time at RC Cola and part time at Red Lobster. The stress of providing for her day-to-day welfare was depleting me of what I needed to give her emotionally and spiritually. God knew that, and this is what He did.

Shortly after my daughter was born, I spotted a White man hitchhiking. I felt obligated to pick him up. Believe it or not, that obligation again went back to the example set by Coach Leggett. Coach had always, and without hesitation, given rides to his Black basketball players. Every day after practice, he'd load up those who needed a ride and take them home. When I saw this man hitchhiking, I knew I needed to help him. It just felt like the right thing to do.

The man and I started talking. He told me that he was working on a job at Washington Square Mall. He also tried to give me $4 for the ride. He said, "Look, I make $8 an hour, and if you hadn't given me a ride, I wouldn't have made a dime." I wouldn't take his money, but I did take all the information I could get from him. Never had I heard of a job that paid $8 an hour. I asked him about his occupation, and he told me he was in the building trade. I knew nothing about this occupation, but I was determined to change that.

My Girls

DeAryon Butler

LeKenya Butler Lawrence

Kaira Butler

Dr. Jokeidré Butler

My Uncle's Support

Uncle Joe suggested that I contact the Black Coalition because they taught Blacks how to apply for jobs in the building trade. I took his advice. Representatives of the coalition showed me the career options available and the corresponding wages. I learned that plumbers made the most per hour. That's all I needed to know. I decided that I wanted to be a plumber.

After the first day, I knew it was the biggest mistake I had ever made in my life. Contemplating my options over the weekend, I revisited memories of unfairness and decided to quit. It wasn't an easy choice. An old nightmare resurfaced, echoing my sophomore year at Gadsden High. This time, it wasn't just my parents; it was my entire family. The world in my mind turned black and white. As the only Black student in the trade, I believed I wouldn't get a fair chance. All the White students seemed at ease, having prior exposure to the trade. Six weeks in, I faced expulsion for failing.

An older Black gentleman offered a piece of advice—if I wanted to be smart, I should emulate smart people. Taking his counsel, I sought help from the class's brightest student, Jeff. He asked a simple question: How many times did I read my lessons? My response— twice. His immediate reply was that I was smarter than him. He read 12 times a night, so I adjusted my approach. Two weeks later, I aced the test.

Excited to share my success with Jeff, I discovered he had been killed three hours earlier in a work accident. His father had asked him to cut a drum that exploded, resulting in Jeff's tragic death at 19. My promise to his father was to be the best. Four years later, I graduated as one of the top plumbers and welders in our class. It was a challenge that reshaped my priorities, marking the first time basketball wasn't a central focus. The journey through the trade was the most arduous experience of my life, especially as it coincided with the government's mandate to integrate the trades. As the sole Black student in my class, I faced name-calling, spitting, nooses hanging, insults about my race and family, and numerous hurtful jokes. Yet, I persevered.

Here is where I received some good news and some bad news. The good news was that the federal government had mandated that the Plumber and Steamfitters Union had to give Blacks a chance. The bad news was that the union only accepted a limited number of Blacks. And if the union agreed to give me a shot by some miracle, I'd have to pass a test. Did I mention that I hated school?

I was old enough to know that nothing about this process would be easy and young enough to have no idea what I was in for. The union was not exactly thrilled with the law offering equal opportunity. To keep up appearances, they accepted a certain number of Blacks to take the test. But to maintain the White majority, I heard the group used the entrance exam to Purdue University as the one *we* had to pass. We didn't know for sure.

Even before this was discovered, those working with the Black Coalition in Evansville knew the deck was stacked against us. However, they had obtained information about what would be included in the test and organized study sessions for us. Initially, I was told that the union had already chosen the two Blacks who would be allowed to take the test. I wasn't one of them. Ultimately, it didn't matter that humans hadn't chosen me because God had.

One of the guys decided not to take the test, and the Black Coalition lobbied for me to fill that spot. The union agreed. I spent the summer of 1976 doing something that I loathed—studying. When I wasn't working or with my family, I was at the office of the Black Coalition preparing for the exam. Finally, it was game time.

In September of that year, I walked into a room with a large group of tight-knit White men. They all knew each other because their fathers, uncles, or relatives had been in the building trade. I was one of two Black men who came to take the exam. And it was hard. It was one of the hardest tests I'd ever taken. Part of the exam involved coordination. Other parts involved drawings that, when folded together, made certain shapes. I was required to know the shapes. It was mind-stretching.

Thankfully, the study sessions had more than prepared me. But I couldn't act like it. I was getting stares from the White men because I'd finish different sections so quickly. To shake off their scrutiny, I started going slower than I needed. That seemed to appease the other test-takers.

Do you get the full impact of how much has changed in our society? Today, men, women, and children, no matter their color or varying abilities, can, without reprisal, take a test as quickly as their skill will allow. Forty years ago, I needed to stay quiet and take a test, drawing no unnecessary attention to myself. In the end, I passed. Okay, I didn't just pass; I aced the test. The Plumber and Steamfitters Union had no choice but to follow through with placing me on a job. I was assigned to ICI Industrial Contractors. While the union obeyed the federal mandate and offered me an opportunity to work in the trade, nothing was forcing them to teach me anything. There wasn't a federal law encouraging them to help me succeed. If anything, they needed me to fail so that I'd quit, and things could go back to the way they were.

The union and its old guard didn't count on three things:

1. I don't quit.
2. I didn't intend to fail.
3. I didn't care if things changed. In fact, change was long overdue. Besides, I had children. I needed this job. I wanted this job. And come what may, I was going to have it! DO IT OR DIE. My first day as an apprentice could have been my last if not for sheer determination. I was assigned to a journeyman at GE who quickly became very frustrated. In his early 30s and not blessed with patience, this

man expected me to know what he knew without actually teaching me anything.

As you can imagine, it didn't go well.

This journeyman would give me an assignment that he thought was simple. I'd never performed even the smallest of these tasks; I had no idea where to begin.

Within the first hour, he was throwing things and screaming at me. The job involved me holding a pipe fitting at just the right angle so he could weld it. These things must line up in a particular way. I'd never done that before, and he didn't offer to show me. My inexperience and his impatience became a cycle of futility.

I'd hold the pipe fitting; he'd weld it. It wouldn't be straight. He'd break it off, throw it, and say, "Go get it."

The process would start all over again. Things went on like this for a while. Finally, he just left me there and went home.

It was my first day, and I was terrified. That fear, coupled with not knowing what I was doing, kept me in a state where I couldn't process or figure out anything. He threw the misshapen pieces, and I brought them back. What else was I supposed to do?

In retrospect, I think he didn't have the patience or the skill to teach someone. Likely, he was afraid to try.

He also expected me to know more than I did. So many apprentices had fathers or other relatives in the business. Therefore, they had some informal training before getting to the apprenticeship stage.

I did not have the same good fortune. However, God provided me with the drive to achieve certain goals while running on nothing but the fuel of determination. My time with Coach Leggett refined this in me.

So, while my first day as an apprentice could have been a bust, I did learn one thing—always wear safety gear.

Around 1 p.m. that first day, my eyes started hurting. By the end of the day, it felt like someone had thrown sand into my eyes, and I rubbed them raw. Driving home, I could barely see.

On the second day of my apprenticeship, I learned why.

While holding the pieces for him to weld, I was supposed to close my eyes or wear a welding hood. I had been looking at the pieces while the welding was underway. My eyes were exposed to the rays from the light of the welding rods.

Another journeyman showed me kindness and let me borrow a welding hood. In that regard, my second day was better. However, my journeyman still yelled, threw things, threatened to have me fired, and went home again. It was unreal!

My third day as an apprentice, well, that's when things really got interesting.

Uncle Ray

Elizabeth Butler Walker

Uncle Joe

Aunt Eula

Come to Jesus

Have you ever been in such an intense situation that time stands still, and the stress of that instance takes your faith—whether you claim to have some or not—to a new level? Some of us call those a "Come to Jesus Moment."

On the third day of my apprenticeship, I had one, thanks to the journeyman, my assignment, and an ominous-looking piece of machinery.

If you haven't picked up on it by now, I was having one heck of a first week. On that third day, the journeyman came into work and told me about my task for the day. Surprisingly, he even threw a few instructions my way. I hardly remember them.

Here's why:

He told me to get into a JLG lift. If you know what that is, understanding will probably dawn on you. If you don't, let me enlighten you.

A JLG lift is a machine with a platform that raises you several feet in the air so you can bypass using a ladder.

The person on the machine drives it. At this point in time, as much as I wished it were otherwise, I was the driver.

As I said earlier, the journeyman gave me a crash course in operations. His parting words were: "Do it wrong, and it will dump you out. Bye."

With Divine assistance, I taught myself to use the machine out of sheer terror. I was beyond scared.

I was moving 25 feet into the air in a box on wheels. If I didn't do it right, it would eject me.

I made it to the sky-high destination. I was to attach hangers. Each hanger was to be 3/8 inch longer than the next one. Sadly, for me and for my easily agitated journeyman, I had no clue what he meant.

Therefore, I did the best that I could, and I attached the hangers.

With me inside, I negotiated the mechanical monster back to the ground. The journeyman said, "You ready to hang pipe?" Then he looked up. Time stood still as he stared at the whopper-jawed pipe hangers, which most definitely didn't meet his specifications. I couldn't tell you how long he stood there looking at my handiwork. As all good things must, his stunned silence ended. He jerked off the welder hood, ripped off his gloves, and shouted, "I can't do this!!!" He grabbed my ruler, snapped it into several pieces, and stormed off. He left. Again.

Although unintentional, his absence was a blessing. I was placed with another journeyman, whom I asked to teach me how to read a ruler. He did. While I appreciated that someone gave me some actual instructions, I was reaching my breaking point.

Tackling the mechanical monster and being asked to perform foreign tasks while dangling 25 feet in the air had taken me to a point, emotionally, that was further than I was willing to go. Or so I thought.

That night, I saw something that, once again, ignited the flame of determination: my little girls. There is no battle that most parents won't fight for their kids. Breaking into the trade was mine.

I took some breaths, grabbed fear by the tail, and reminded myself that I'd studied math. I could do this.

I returned to work on the fourth day of my apprenticeship. I had no trouble measuring anything. That day, my gem of a journeyman gave me the closest thing to a compliment I'd ever receive from him. He said, "Well, you must have gone to school last night."

Out of the Frying Pan, Into the Fire

I NEVER THOUGHT THAT I'D LOOK BACK ON THAT SURLY JOURNEYMAN WITH ANYTHING BUT RELIEF THAT MY TIME WITH HIM WAS OVER. I was 20 and horribly wrong.

On my fifth day as an apprentice, I was told to report to Alcoa. Problem number one: I had no idea where that was. Problem number two: I figured my reception by the Alcoa employees couldn't be any worse than what I'd just experienced.

The answer to my first problem was simple enough. I asked my father-in-law for directions on how to get to Alcoa. The answer to my second problem didn't come to me for many years. But it did come.

My introduction to my new job site started smoothly enough. I went to the guard shack, was told where to go, and joined the other pipefitters. Besides me, there was one other Black man. He was an older gentleman, but I was relieved to see a face the same color as mine. That feeling was fleeting. I learned quickly that he wasn't an ally. He kept his job the only way he knew how—by making fun of his race and being the butt of the White man's jokes.

As a new apprentice, I was to be assigned to a journeyman. I remember all the White journeymen lined the walls inside the building where we assembled. The supervisor came in, faced them, and asked, "Okay. Who wants the n-word?" Yes, he was referring to me. One by one, each man shook his head no. I stood there, as time after time, with just one word, I was rejected based on nothing more than my color.

Finally, a man with the apprenticeship board said he'd take me. The supervisor looked at him and said, "If he f*cks up, get rid of him."

My new journeyman looked at me and said, "Come on, n-word. Let's go."

The day didn't get better. I don't think he even used my name, first or last. I was just "n-word" or other equally foul names.

The stress of the situation caused me to disappear into myself. I felt nothing and moved like I was in a trance.

Believe it or not, that shock may have been God's gift in a horrifically evil situation created by men.

I know you probably think I'm crazy. But in this place, void of emotion, I was protected from something that could've been my downfall—reacting. After being paired, the journeyman and I left the shack and headed to the designated job site within the plant. Once at the site, I was approached by another White man who handed me a piece of paper. I glanced at it and saw these words: "Application for N-Word Employment."

At the top of the page, it said: "Photos are not necessary since you all look alike."

They all stood around and laughed at me while I shoved the paper into my pocket. I didn't read the rest until I got home. It's been more than 30 years, but I still remember every word on that page.

1. What's the number one desire of a n-word? To have a White woman.
2. Why do n-word have Cadillacs? The glove compartments are big enough to carry watermelons.
3. What's another name for a Cadillac? A coon cage.
4. How do you babysit a n-word baby? Lick their lips and stick them to a wall.
5. How can you tell if a n-word is in the area? Rib bones and watermelon seeds.
6. When is the best time to catch a n-word? First of the month at the mailbox when they get food stamps.
7. How do n-words get sickle cell anemia? By licking food stamps.

8. Why do n-words have chickens in the yard? To teach them how to walk.
9. What do you call two n-words in a shoe box? A pair of loafers.
10. What's a good n-word? A dead one.

It's awful, isn't it? Thankfully, nearly 20 years into the 21st century, most men and women never come close to dealing with this type of abuse. It's no longer a social norm but a social evil.

In the 1970s, it was a different story. That night at home, I read this "application" and did the only thing I could—I went back to work. Don't get me wrong. I was angry. I hated the actions of these ridiculous, ignorant men. I was hurt and dreaded with everything in me the idea of facing them again, of enduring them again.

I learned that other Black men had fought back and were kicked out of the apprenticeship. That wasn't going to be me. Come hell or high water, I was going to break into this business and make a good living for my kids. I was going to carve out my own spot in a profession dominated by White men. I was going to forge a path for other Black men and women who might want to do the same thing.

So, I made a choice. I chose to keep going, to learn everything I could, and to not let them beat me.

Esther, Joseph, Me, and You

BULLY—a bad person, one who doesn't like themselves, a blustering, browbeating person; one habitually cruel to others who are weak and afraid.

EVIL—a heartless, gutless person trying to cause harm; morally reprehensible, brings sorrow, distress, and calamity.

THERE ARE MANY DIFFERENT WORDS THAT DESCRIBE THE SAME ACTIONS. Bully/evil are interchangeable. Both try the same thing—to break your spirit. When the first shot doesn't do it, the bully or person operating in a place of evil escalates. If there's anything you can count on, a bully will try again. The bullies at my new job site tried again, and it's by the grace of God that I'm here to even tell you about it.

But before I write any more about them, I want to tell you about two people who could empathize with me and me with them. Both lives are recorded in the Bible, which I believe is the Word of God and is true.

Esther was a young Jewess made queen of a foreign land at a time when her husband had given the order to annihilate her people. She chose her course and risked her head—literally—to approach the king to request mercy.

Joseph was sold as a slave by his brothers. He ended up in a country far from home. As with most slaves, he might not have even spoken the language of those giving him orders. After arriving in this new land and being placed as a servant, Joseph made a choice. He chose to be a hard worker and honest man who honored God. For that, he found himself a foreign slave in a foreign land and confined to a foreign prison. But only for a time.

By trusting God in the unjust circumstances, Joseph was eventually elevated to second in command of the country.

By trusting God, even in the face of death, Esther helped her people survive a slaughter.

The majority of folks surrounding Esther and Joseph were not their friends. Both lived in times of great prejudice and powerlessness because of their race and socioeconomic class.

Both were given the opportunity by God to orchestrate change. All they had to do was choose.

Esther 4:14b says, "… And who knows but that you have come to a royal position for such a time as this" (ESV).

In Genesis 50:19–20, Joseph told his brothers, "Don't be afraid. Am I in the place of God? You intended to harm me, but God intended it for good to accomplish what is now being done, the saving of many lives."

And then there's me … and you.

In some ways, I'm better off than Esther and Joseph. I live in America, where laws are in place to protect me from slavery and my race, all races and religions, from annihilation. The laws also protect my human right to work for any dream I want to see fulfilled.

When White men didn't want me in their building trade, I was told to go start my own trade, my own business. So I did.

Being treated with respect and dignity are the innate rights of all who are created in the image of God, but ultimately, it can't be forced. There is no legislation that can govern a human heart. There are also no laws that can dictate the human heart's response to ugliness and bigotry. It comes down to who you want to be and your subsequent actions to become that person.

There have been and still are many doors closed in my face because I'm Black. I know what's out there, and there's no fight. If this is my house, then I bring in who I want. Some companies bring in people who look like them to do the job. You're going to have a struggle in life. If you find yourself in such a situation—go in and change it. I could have cried racism, but instead, I learned everything I could and then started my own company.

And just like others, I decide who comes into my house.

Nothing is holding you back but you. So the questions are: What do you want? And who do you want to be?

What I Didn't Know

IT TAKES A GREAT DEAL OF EFFORT TO BRING LIFE INTO THIS WORLD AND SURPRISINGLY LITTLE TO TAKE IT OUT. It can be as easy as dropping an object from a certain height when your target is several floors below you.

I work in the building/trade industry. Injuries and death due to falling/dropped objects are occupational hazards and tragic accidents. Unfortunately, in my case, it wasn't an accident.

After receiving the "Application for N-Word Employment," I returned to work, completely unsure of what to do. I wasn't wanted there; I didn't want to be there, but being there could open doors to a new life for my girls and me. In my mind then and now, choosing what to do was easy. How to do it was another matter.

I kept thinking about Coach, a man I once hated and a man I believed had it out for me. When I compared him to my new coworkers, I was astounded to see how good he was to me. I never saw racism in him. And he could've been so much worse because we were farther south.

Back at Alcoa, my boss told the journeyman to put me on a boiler to tighten some pieces. The boiler was right next to the power plant. At first, I didn't know that I was being watched. Then suddenly, a can fell from several stories up and hit near me. Then another. And another. They kept getting closer and closer.

Finally, a supervisor said, "Go get the n-word before they kill him."

At the time, I didn't get how serious the situation was. I knew they hated me; I felt that. But I saw them like I would high school bullies during a dodgeball game. I might get hit, but nobody dies during dodgeball. My 26-year-old mind didn't grasp what was happening.

Perhaps that, and the fact that I wasn't killed, were examples of God's grace.

Forty years later, all pretense is gone. I see now that I was in real danger. Had I known then what I know now, I would've left and never looked back. I would have let the door close on innumerable opportunities. I would have left and given them exactly what they wanted.

But I didn't leave.

You see, I wanted something. I wanted to make the team. In those days, Black people just survived. Most of us didn't plan for our future or look forward to a certain profession the way a White person could. We weren't allowed to think that way. We weren't encouraged to believe in ourselves or view ourselves as human beings with the right to dream.

I started to parallel my goal of becoming a journeyman with my objective to make the basketball team in high school. I knew that my bosses at Alcoa were nothing like my high school coach. My coach saw me as a human being created in the image of God. The Alcoa bosses saw me as just another Black. Their hearts were remarkably different.

The challenge was before me. I needed to make the team to move forward. Truthfully, after they tried to discourage me and I realized what I was up against, I wasn't sure I wanted to play their game anymore.

Nevertheless, I didn't leave. Instead, I decided to change the game. I could because I'd done it before when I played basketball. I just needed to watch my opponent, learn their moves, and stay one step ahead.

Game on!

How NBA Players Taught Me the Trade

Every Sunday, I had a date. The day of rest before another grueling work week was my day to watch the NBA and absorb what I saw from the game I loved.

Jerry West, better known as Mr. Clutch, taught me a lot about defense and stopping on a dime for a jump shot. Earl Monroe, AKA the Pearl, was a guard I tried to mimic, especially his spin moves and his ability to pass. Finally, there was Oscar Robinson, or the Big O. He had a certain pizazz with assists and actually led the NBA in assists and points for an entire season.

I watched these athletes faithfully because of my time with Coach Leggett. Until I was brought under his wing, I played a selfish game. Coach Leggett told me that that kind of game was for the playground, but I had to know so much more as a team player. He wanted me to hone my skills in everything from scoring, passing, rebounding, and defensive plays, as well as how to follow his instructions. I was short in high school, so I had to work that much harder. My Sunday dates with the NBA helped me. I watched the game and then practiced the moves I saw until I mastered them.

Not too many years later, I still needed to learn from the masters. At Alcoa, I noticed several team leaders who stood out—Bill Zimmer, Steve Sitzman, and Mike Water.

Zimmer was considered one of the best welders. He was so respected at Alcoa that they refused to test his welds. This was unheard of. He was my Jerry West.

Sitzman could manage a job and keep everyone in line. I admired his management skills. He was my Earl Monroe.

Water, my Oscar Robinson, was a great plumber. He often used the n-word. His use of that word incited in me something else—pride. I don't mean the type that comes with the confidence of knowing and respecting yourself. I'm referring to the pride that is mostly arrogance and leads you to fall flat on your face.

That type of pride wasn't going to teach me anything. But watching these men and being educated by them, despite them, would teach me a great deal. A terrific battle raged inside me. Do I focus on the hurt feelings and rebellion from being treated as less than human? Or do I turn the tables by learning everything I could and using their skills to do it?

Steve Sitzman

To Beat Them, Join Them

IT'S BEEN SAID IF YOU CAN'T BEAT THEM, JOIN THEM. This was true for me with a slight variation. I *knew* I could beat them, but I needed to join them long enough to learn *how*.

I knew who the MVPs of the trade were, and I had to have their knowledge. That's when I started borrowing the blueprints of our jobs. In basketball, you have strategies to win. That's why a coach develops plays and keeps them in his playbook.

The journeymen I worked with had their playbooks, or blueprints, from which I needed to study and learn.

Initially, I didn't plan to borrow the blueprints. But one day, at the end of the shift, I was in the restroom with the other workers, washing the dirt and grime from our hands. One of the White guys started laughing at me and said, "How do you n-words know when your hands are clean?"

I shot back, "We just run the water until it's clear coming off our hands." After this exchange, I walked out of the bathroom. And that's when I spotted the blueprints. It was like a lightning bolt hit me! I knew these would be part of my playbook, so I took them.

I folded them tight, stuck them in the back of my pants, and pulled my shirttail out over them. That night, I took them home and studied them. I was working with this journeyman to install bathrooms. By following the plans, I could visualize how everything was set up in the bathrooms in which we were working. The next day, I went to work early and slid them back into the box where the journeyman had put them.

At first, I wasn't 100 percent sure the way I was interpreting the plans was accurate. Therefore, the next day, when the journeyman started the same routine: "What's this measurement? What's that measurement?" I said, "I don't know."

He said, "That's why n-words can't learn! That's why n-words are stupid!"

At the end of the day, I retrieved the plans just as I'd done the day before. I took them home and studied them. I did this for several days in a row.

I started remembering the dimensions he requested. Finally, I got bold. I was ready for him.

One day, he came in smiling. As usual, he was with a group of White men, and they were fully prepared to laugh at me. He said, "What's that measurement n-word?"

I said, "That's 17 percent."

Then he said, "What's that one?"

I said, "That's 25 and a half."

At this point, he stopped talking and started pointing. He'd point, and I'd rattle off the measurements.

Each time he asked a question, and I had the answer, he'd get a little angrier. With each correct response, he started puffing and blowing—angry that I knew what I was talking about. He was trying, and failing, to figure out how I had learned to read the measurements.

Until that moment, he was secure in his belief that Black people weren't as intelligent or as capable as White people. He had even been trying to program me to fit the image *he* had of Black people. For a while, it worked. Then, I started taking the drawings.

Every evening before he went home, he'd set the plans inside the toolbox, leaving the box open while he went to wash his hands. As an apprentice, it was my job to lock the box, which I did. But I'd take the plans first. There was a dummy lock where I could leave one end unlocked.

After I got home from work, helped with the kids, and did other things around the house, I'd study the drawings. I'd spend about two hours each night studying the measurements and blueprint layouts.

In the mornings, I'd go to work, lift the side I'd left unlocked, and slide the plans in.

The extra study time worked! The day I stepped up and showed him what I knew, that's the day things started changing.

After correctly answering his questions and making him angry, I remembered that he folded the drawings and put them in his pocket. Obviously, he wanted to keep the plans close so that I couldn't see them. He and several other White men at the job site believed that all Blacks were thieves. He was convinced that I was somehow taking the drawings during the day. He never thought that I was borrowing them at night and studying them.

His ability to underestimate me opened the door for me to prove them all wrong, so I didn't verbally try to correct his ignorance. In his mind, there was no way I could be seeing the drawings. They were locked up at night and guarded by him all day.

He didn't realize that telling me I was stupid and couldn't think backfired on him. It made me think. It made me grab the opportunity to study those drawings. Soon, it wasn't about him; it was about me. He was building me, making me a better apprentice, and he couldn't even see it!

I worked with him for another few months. He was abusive until the end, and he never figured out how I was becoming more skilled.

Eventually, I was moved to work with another journeyman at Alcoa. I'd worked with him before, and I knew what to expect. He was about image. He liked believing he was a great teacher. I'd already learned the blueprints. I knew how this guy wanted to be perceived; the rest was easy.

He started just like the rest—a name-caller. He'd say derogatory things about my kids whenever he had an audience. A representative of the Black Coalition had warned me that the union would try to force me out.

That wasn't going to happen.

Instead, I adopted the attitude that silence is golden and let him lead. Then, one day, I asked him if I could run the job of building the bathroom—from the blueprints to the final faucet. I reminded him that he'd been preparing me for just such an opportunity. He seemed to appreciate himself for that because he let me take charge of the job.

Up to this point, the journeyman had a pet phrase he used with me. He'd say, "Get your head out of your a**, n-word, and let's go."

Since I was now in charge, I looked at him and said, "Get your head out of your a**, and let's go…" To say the least, he was shocked. I quickly assured him that I was playing. He believed me.

This journeyman was indeed a piece of work. Yet, I knew I'd been given a great opportunity by running my first job, and I wasn't about to blow it.

I knew how to read blueprints and install a bathroom, but I still asked him questions so that he believed I needed him. He bought it and kept instructing me. In his mind, I was catching on "real fast" thanks to his teaching.

There's a trick to sports. If you figure out the players, you can win the game. It's the same with life. And at this moment, I'd figured them out. I started standing a little taller because I knew I could do this.

This journeyman started liking me simply because I benefited him. Here's how.

Normally, it would take three days to complete a bathroom. It was now taking only a day and a half. We probably put in 25 bathrooms. Once we cut our time down, we'd go to the vending machine; he would buy ice cream, and we'd sit and talk for a day and a half. He'd do most of the talking. I wouldn't say anything because it would give him fuel to use against me later.

Those were some pretty relaxing days. This was our routine until the day we got caught.

Sleeping on the Job Has Its Benefits

TODAY, I AM MY OWN BOSS. I employ people and expect them to work hard at whatever task they are assigned. I would never approve of a nap during the workday.

Thirty years ago, I didn't get to nap as an apprentice. Instead, I was the lookout. Sort of.

One day, the journeyman and I got a job done early. My journeyman said, "I'll take a nap, and you watch; then I'll watch while you take a nap."

Unfortunately, I'm not a good lookout. We both fell asleep. And that's how the boss found us.

Talk about an awkward few minutes.

The boss really wanted to be mad at us, but he couldn't say anything since we'd completed the job.

After we slid past his wrath, my journeyman said to me, "I should've known better than to leave a n-word on watch." Yes, he was still saying that word, but the emotion behind it was changing.

Attitude Turns to Opportunity

Once I knew how to play the game, my attitude changed, and more opportunities began presenting themselves. One day, my journeyman told me he was going on vacation. Not knowing what to do with me, they initially decided to make me work with the previous apprentice (who still hadn't figured out how I managed to study those blueprints).

When I discovered their plan, I asked if they'd let me work alone. I knew I could run a job by myself and requested that I be allowed to.

The journeyman said, "You can't. You're an apprentice."

I said, "But you taught me well." His prowess as an educator convinced him, and he went to the boss on my behalf.

The boss was skeptical. "An apprentice and a n-word?"

The journeyman said, "No, he's pretty sharp, and I taught him well."

That argument either convinced my boss, or he saw what he thought was a "legitimate" opportunity to get rid of me. The boss said, "Okay, but if he screws up, he's gone!"

The pressure was on. This boss, perhaps even gleefully, believed I'd be gone by the time my journeyman returned.

My journeyman had enough sense to feel some pressure, too. He said, "You better not let me down."

I said, "I won't."

And I didn't.

I wasn't there, so I don't know for sure, but I doubt that journeyman relaxed much on his vacation.

He was gone a week, and he knew his boss would have plenty to say if I didn't perform every task to their standards.

Counselor, Great Physician... and Plumber

G OD IS ALL THINGS. He is all-powerful. He is all-knowing. He is everywhere. That week, He was by my side at every water fountain and bathroom at Alcoa.

The first day by myself, the boss sent me to install a water fountain. This was something I'd never done before—ever. I had no idea where to begin. That's when I did the best thing anyone can do in any situation.

I started praying. It was one mile from the point where I received my assignment to the actual job site on the Alcoa property.

I spent that one-mile bike ride talking to the Almighty. God spoke back. He told me to find a drinking fountain and see how it's put together. I took His advice. When I looked at a water fountain, I discovered that it was easy to install. I put in the new water fountain in less than 20 minutes.

Instead of reporting back, I knew there were other bathrooms to finish. I made an executive decision to go from job to job and get things done. That day, I went to various bathrooms and set the toilets, installed mirrors, and completed what we in the trade call "the finish work." I was gone for four hours before reporting back; I rode my bike back to the shack to face the boss. When he saw me, he started cursing me. He thought I'd spent four hours on a water fountain. (Mind you, he didn't come looking to see if I was doing okay or needed help.) He just kept yelling, "Why did I let a n-word go by himself?!"

When his rant subsided somewhat, he ordered, "Take your a** to building 16 and put that hot water tank in."

Very calmly, I said, "It's done."

Then he yelled at me, demanding that I go and finish a certain bathroom.

I said, "It's done."

His voice started changing. For the first time since he started screaming at me, he turned around and looked me in the eye.

"Get in my truck," he said.

He drove to every location, looked at every completed job, and drove back to the shack.

That's when he said, "Butler, kid, you're a hell of a mechanic!"

Then he said, "Go home with pay for the rest of the day. Son, you deserve it."

That was a big deal. The next thing that happened was that he gave *me* an apprentice. I was a second-year apprentice with an apprentice. That was unheard of!

When the engineers came for an inspection, one complained that a drain was 1/8 inch too tall. So my boss stepped on it, pushed it down 1/8 of an inch, and said, "Okay, Butler, let's go." After that inspection, we went back to the shack, where we got our assignments each day. He said, "Your journeyman will be back tomorrow. No wonder he wants to keep you."

I said, "Yes, he's taught me a lot."

At this point, I felt like I'd just scored the winning basket. I was now Mr. Clutch. From that point on, I started elevating higher and higher.

The Next Level

I'D REACHED A MOUNTAINTOP IN MY CAREER, BUT IT WAS ONLY THE BEGINNING.

While I'd accomplished my first major career goal, I'm not the sort to set up camp and get comfortable there.

It wasn't long before I noticed White employees getting overtime, but I wasn't. I was married with two children who insisted on eating several times daily, so I needed the money.

I did some investigating and was told that plumbers didn't get overtime, but welders did. However, I knew that some White plumbing apprentices were getting overtime.

The next level had been determined. In some of my plumbing classes, we received some instruction in welding, but I needed more to certify myself as a welder.

You're probably wondering why welding became so important to me. Well, let me put it into dollars and cents.

At this time, all the overtime was double time. A regular welder made $600 a week, plus 44 hours of overtime. Welders were making $2,000 a week as a journeyman—that was five times what I was making. As a plumbing apprentice, I was making $360 a week.

I approached an instructor at a pipefitters and plumbing union hall where we had classes at night. I asked him if he'd open the school so that I could practice welding. He asked when.

I said, "Every day and every night. Every night but Sunday." He was a little hesitant.

"I'm not supposed to," he said. But by the grace of God, he did. He opened it every day except Sunday and on holidays for me to practice.

Every day after work, I practiced. Every Saturday, I practiced. I practiced welding every day except for Sunday.

Eight weeks after my self-imposed tutorial, I was ready to inform my employers of my newly acquired skill.

Ready, Set, Go

ALCOA HAD WHAT'S CALLED A ROLLING MILL. They used a new system that required X-ray welds to join pipes together. An X-ray weld is where you join the metals together with no flaws. They called the Union Hall, asking for welders.

My time had come. I stepped up and let them know I could weld.

Had I not been living and thriving under a regime of people who constantly underestimated me, I might have wilted from their response.

They said, "You can't weld." They even tried to prove it to me.

The foreman sent me to the shop to take a test. Some would fail that test, and they were hoping I'd be one of them.

I'm not going to lie. I was afraid. I'd faithfully studied and practiced the art of welding, but I was still scared.

On the way to the test, I started singing to myself what, in actuality, was a cry for help and a song of praise: "God, hold my hand, and God, guide my hand to make the weld."

He did, and I passed.

Now, the bosses had no choice but to put me on the welding job.

Welding requires certain protective equipment beyond what a plumber needs. I needed a specific type of gloves and leather sleeves to protect my hands and arms from the welding-flame sparks. I didn't have either. My supervisor took gloves off a White man's hands and gave them to me. He gave the White welder a brand-new set of gloves. He did not, however, get me any leather sleeves.

He knew I needed them. I knew I needed them, but I had to forge ahead. Do you know that 30 years later, I still bear the scars from where I was burned by the welding sparks?

Finally, the supervisor took the leather sleeves off the same White welder and gave them to me.

He gave the White man new leather sleeves.

As for the job itself, I was assigned to the hardest welds to make.

Again, I was nervous. Instead of letting that emotion rule me, I did what any believer should do. I prayed and asked God for His help to succeed in making a great weld.

At night, supervisors would come in to X-ray the welds. They'd fire you or kick you off the job if they were bad. There was no wiggle room and no second chances, especially for a Black man who wanted the same opportunity for overtime as White men.

They X-rayed my work and determined I had no bad welds. At that moment, I was able to exhale a little bit.

Getting close to the end of the job, all of us welders were extremely tired. I'm not sure what the schedule was for the White welders, but I was working 16-hour days. I'd go home for a bit of sleep and be back to weld again.

I was welding so much that I made $2,100 that week. The money was great, but the cost in terms of exhaustion was high. I'd find myself falling asleep during a weld. However, God's favor was on me, and all of my welds were determined to be good.

The last two days of the job were the hardest stretch. It was all day, paid double time, and no one went home. I still didn't have any bad welds. That fact began to circulate, and one of the other welders nicknamed me Zero because I had zero bad welds.

After completing the welds, I made a promise to myself. Right then, I decided that I'd be the best plumber and welder to come out of my class. I wanted to do it for me, my family, and my friend Scotty.

Scotty was one of my fellow classmates learning the trade. He taught me how to study, which ultimately kept me from failing. Scotty was killed on a job, so I couldn't express to him my deep gratitude. I wanted to earn the top spot in the class to thank his father for the kindness Scotty had shown me.

I wanted to win the best in the class award at graduation and hand it to Scotty's father. In my mind, there was no doubt that he would have won the award for our class.

As part of the graduation requirements, we were tested. Part of my test involved welding. You had to weld things that were purposefully located in very difficult positions without adjusting anything.

Two of the guys I tested with rolled the welds to finish the tasks more easily. They tried to convince me to do the same, but I refused. I wanted to finish the test honestly and win the award based on merit.

I came in third. Only God knows who really won. My class graduated in 1980. I was officially a plumbing journeyman and a certified welder. I'd done it!

Bill Hastie

Bruce Pellum

Looking Back

I'D REACHED ANOTHER PINNACLE, AND IT WAS TIME AGAIN TO REFLECT. I looked at the game of basketball. Some people think that what I endured was terrible. It was, and it wasn't. You see, in basketball, you have an official, a coach, who oversees the players on the court. And my official was and is God. God makes all the calls, and you don't have to do anything except follow His direction. I thrived during the game and did not earn technical fouls because I let the official make the call.

Some people may say a ref made a bad call, but if you win at the end of the game, it doesn't matter about that call. I looked at the coach. The coach is supposed to direct you, and you're supposed to go through the plays. My role was to do whatever the coach put before me. My job was to work hard and learn the plays, and I started looking at basketball players. A lot of the great Black players got traded, and the great White players weren't ever traded. It taught me that when you are playing on someone else's team, they have the right to do whatever they think will make the most money.

At the time, I was looking at it like the Black players were getting mistreated, but as the owner of the team, it was his right to do what he felt was best. I realized that if I went into business for myself, I'd have the same right. It takes a lot of guts and effort to go out on your own; it gives you the right to make the call. If I went out on my own, I could make the call. So, I started looking at going into business for myself. Then, I thought about living at home in Tennessee. When we were making flower beds, we'd go get chicken manure. With the right amount, the plants grew. I looked back on the guys who gave me such a hard time; they were manure, and they fertilized me well. I grew up strong and am now producing, thanks to all the manure.

As a human being created in the image of God, the Alcoa bosses saw me as just another Black. Their hearts were remarkably different.

The challenge was before me. I needed to make the team to move forward.

If Anyone in This World Can Make It, It's You

IT WAS 1989, AND I HAD BEEN IN KENTUCKY DOING PROJ-ECTS FOR A YEAR OR MORE. Finally, in my mind, all things seemed to be running smoothly. Unfortunately, I now managed a crew of all-White men in the state of Kentucky after being moved there to take on a new customer. They needed someone to come do a small job which was supposed to last about three weeks. After meeting the president of the company, I was able to persuade him to get in a lift with a welding hood to watch me weld and compare my welding to the existing company he had hired. After watching, he was convinced my welding was superior to the ones he was using; therefore, he had them leave the job, and I took over all construction at his site. At this point, he allowed the company that I worked for to take on bigger projects at his plant, and I added more men to the project.

I noticed the desolation of pumps and piping. I once again went to the president and explained how they would have a problem with the pumps; he allowed me to disconnect the pump and install it the correct way. After this, he gave me the whole plant. He said, "You will take over all projects now. This plant has gone from non-union to union."

The next day, the president visited the company next door and explained to them the work I was doing. The company next door allowed me to come to their plant to start doing work. I was able to bring more people to complete these jobs, so I then had two crews of men working with me. My boss was very pleased with the progress I was making in Kentucky. Then, they allowed me to take on a third company. They seemed to be very pleased; we were performing at a high level on all three jobs. The Union Hall was pleased because we were putting more people to work. Three plants that employed non-union workers had now become unionized.

After doing this for a year or more, I was told, with no explanation, that they needed certified welders at a plant called Alcoa. I had graduated as a plumber but had learned to weld and was a certified welder. In my mind, everything was running smoothly.

Then, I got a call from my supervisor to come to the office. He said, "I need you to go to Alcoa on Monday. Someone else will be taking over these jobs. You will go from a supervisor to a welder." They had decided, for some unknown reason, that they wanted me to go to Alcoa and weld.

I simply asked, "Why? I'm running these jobs over here. Everyone seemed to be happy, so why do I have to leave this?"

He said, "Like it or not, you will go to Alcoa on Monday." I was not happy, so I went to see the owner. Once I was inside the owner's office, he said, "Lawrence, I like you; you know I've always liked you. But once the business agent in Kentucky found out you were Black, you were called dumb f**king n-word every day, and this is why we want you to go to Alcoa Monday morning."

I replied, "How do you feel about me going back to Alcoa to weld?"

He said, "We need you there. You are a very good welder. Lawrence, I think the world of you. And you're a good person, but we need welders."

I asked him, "How long has this been going on?"

He said, "Ever since we sent you to Kentucky."

I said, "So, it was never a problem before, and now it is since you need welders." I looked him in his eyes and said, "I've spent all these years in the apprenticeship being called and treated like a n-word. I trained White boys in this company. You gave them all brand new trucks and gave me the ragged one in the company. Yet, I never complained. I worked on weekends for free to make sure we had work in this company, and you're telling me it doesn't matter. I quit!"

I went back to my supervisor next door. I took his truck keys out of my pocket and said, "I'll go back to Tennessee, and I'll dig in the dirt before I'll ever be your n-word again." I threw the keys across the table in his direction, walked out, and looked up with tears of fear and shame running down my face. I said, "God, I'm Yours."

I called my wife to come pick me up. After she arrived, I told her what had happened. She said, "If anyone in this world can make it, it is you." We didn't have any money. "I will work," she said. "And we will work this out together. I believe in you."

I sat silently while tears poured down my face. I asked her to take me to Union Hall. After arriving at Union Hall, I asked for the business agent. When he looked at me, he could tell something was wrong. I explained to him what had happened. He said if I did not like it, I could come back over there. I had no choice. I looked at him, and once again, tears started to flow. I said, "I come to the Union Hall meetings and listen to the officers tell their Black jokes and never say a word." I took out my union card, and he said, "Think about what you're doing."

I told him, "I quit. You can have this union card and all the people that represent it. I quit." Then I walked out. While walking out, I said, "Thirteen years of my life I have given to this trade, and I'm still being called a n-word. No more! No more! No more!"

In order to change people, you must first change yourself. My change was that I was not going to be his n-word. I went back to the job site and asked the president of the company if he would give me a few minutes, which he did. I said, "I have been called a n-word. I have had plenty of years of hearing it; you would think I would be used to it by now. If I started my own business, can I start right here?"

He said, "Absolutely; you can finish this job." I told him that I had three problems, and I hoped he could help me with two of them. He said he couldn't promise anything, but he would try. One, I couldn't afford to hire a man. He immediately replied, "I will get one from your competitor." Two, I couldn't afford any equipment to weld. He immediately replied that there was a welding machine in the plant I could use. Three was on me. I only had $2,500 to my name, a wife, and four children.

I set up a meeting that afternoon with Score, where there were eight businessmen in the company who would advise you on what you needed to start a business. After meeting with them, all eight of them told me I needed $250,000. I asked them who would loan a Black man $250,000. One of them said, "You asked, and we're telling you. You will fail before you start." One man took a pen, stuck it in his mouth, and leaned back in his chair. He said, "Our plates are full." I got up and walked out.

I went home and received a phone call later that afternoon. It was the secretary of the company I reported to. She asked me to meet her that afternoon at Pizza Hut on Washington Avenue at about 5:30. She said, "I heard them saying today that you had quit, and they were laughing." She asked me what I was going to do. I told her I was going into business for myself. She told me she knew some of the things that would help me that I didn't know. She met me to give them to me. I asked, "Why are you helping me?"

She said, "I feel bad. The whole year you were coming up there, didn't you notice that there was another White man that was coming into the shack before you came in?" She stated that she was told she shouldn't be alone with a n-word and that she felt she was a part of everything that happened. So, she met me with papers to show me how to bill and charge.

She said jokingly, "You know your price is going to have to be cheaper than theirs."

"Hopefully not." I told her I would have to buy a truck. She advised me on how to charge for the truck, and then we parted ways. While looking at the information she gave me, I quickly realized I could maximize the $2,500. First, I bought a truck for $1,500. I had to carry cardboard in the truck to put beneath it because it leaked oil so badly. I did not want to leave stains on anyone's driveway. I used the truck as one of my tools and charged $500 a week for the truck, and I quickly got my money back.

The employee sourced from a competitor's shop assisted me with tasks, though not happily. While we worked, a co-worker shouted out, "How does it feel to work for a n-word?" I only used him for metal tacking during the day, as he wouldn't help me do anything else.

When the president left for home, I went home briefly, only to return to work and go on until the late hours, sometimes until 2 or 3 a.m., with occasional help from my wife. I returned at 5 a.m., driven by determination.

The president noticed and came by and said, "You're getting a lot of work done." I told him I would get more done if I had my own man. He casually suggested I hire someone myself. I assumed he forgot that I didn't have the money for that. I turned in my invoice for the week, and as I walked out, the secretary stopped me. I was afraid I'd done something wrong. To my surprise, they issued a check on the spot.

There was a project manager, a White man, positioned under the president. He approached me three weeks into my work, informing me that I would have to turn all of my invoices to him. He assured me he had submitted my invoice to the office, and he shared that he had increased my $500 invoice to $1,500, asserting that I owed him $1,000 as a consultant's fee. When I asked him about this, he said, "Because I am the project manager, and that's how this works around here." This was all new to me, so I did what I thought was best and kept my mouth shut.

I had a big job coming up, and I asked for $5,000 for material. To my surprise, he came to my house and said the president wanted to see me the following morning. I asked why, only to learn that he had increased the invoice to $15,000, saying, "There is a $10,000 consultant's fee."

Not knowing what to do and being new to running my own business, I confided in my wife. Her advice was clear: tell the president. I said, "I'm a black cat, and they are all white dogs. Who is going to believe a black cat? I will automatically be wrong." I was afraid I would lose the business before it even started.

So, I went off by myself to think and pray. The first thing that came to mind was what I'd done wrong that I had yet to ask forgiveness for. The only thing I could remember was stealing from a little store where I grew up in Tennessee called the Red Store. For some reason, it never left my mind.

Then I thought about how no matter what you do in life, you have more than one White man to go through. Among 10, the likelihood of finding even two who genuinely support or prioritize your success, particularly if you're perceived as beneath them, is slim. It seemed irrelevant whether you stood tall at 6-foot-10; as long as they towered over you at 6-foot-10 and a half, your achievements held little significance. It was like one could never succeed—there were too many to go through, and it only took one to stop you.

I recalled a White man who helped when no Black person supported me. I remembered when I was going through the trade without any clothes. A White man saw me and bought me clothes. If it hadn't been for basketball, I wouldn't have had a jacket at all. I thought about how I wanted to learn to weld, and a White man opened the school so I could practice at night, on weekends, and even on holidays.

I remembered how some of the White men were treated poorly and realized they could empathize with my feelings. This led me to recall my previous employment and how the owner never even worked in this field. He was always so polite and treated me like a man, but he didn't realize the mistreatment I endured from those he appointed above me. Most of them had no use for a Black man. I had no choice but to take whatever they handed out due to their positions appointed by the owners. I had no freedom.

My life has been like living in a zoo with all the limitations put on the animals. They were no longer free to be what they were created to be. People pay money to see them. They could never feel or hear what the animal had to say. The animal's only hope was that someone would pay attention, but people couldn't care less about its behavior. They were paying to see it perform, not to see how it felt or understand its feelings. Plus, the man at the top only cared about getting his money.

You have no way of telling anyone your true pain, and all you hoped is that someone would notice beyond your skin color or behavior. It only takes the right person, and your whole life can change for the better. And it only takes one bad person for your whole life to stop and never get a chance to take off.

Then I thought about what I had said to a White man one day. I asked him how he would feel being the only White man in the world with everyone else being Black. He told me he would never have to worry about that because the White man would always be in charge.

Finally, I remembered the one White man who treated me like an animal. After three weeks of his prejudice towards me, he expressed astonishment that despite his mistreatment, I had never shown him a bad attitude. He hugged me and cried and said he would never judge another Black man; he'd only done what he was taught. I hugged him and cried. I told him I had a greater job to do. I said, "If I don't show you different than what you were taught, you have no way of showing anyone else."

I returned my thoughts back to my existing problem—how to tell the boss that he had placed a bad guy over me. The project he had given me was a $140,000 project. I knew I had to explain to him the next morning why my invoice was $15,000 when I was just starting the job and hadn't gotten much done. I called the guy that I knew had a machine shop and moved all my material to his machine shop at 11:00 that night.

The next morning, I approached work without any sleep. All I could think of was him waiting for me to come in. He was visibly angry. He told me to show him $15,000 worth of work. While riding to the fabricating shop, I prayed in my head and finally got an answer.

I looked at the president and said, "I know $15,000 seems like a lot of money, but you won't have to pay any more to cover this project." I told him the $15,000 would cover the project. He was happy, and why wouldn't he be? His $140,000 project just turned into a $15,000 one. I had to make it work. I worked day and night for free to get the project out. Some nights, my wife would come out and help me with the projects. I was able to get it done. I feel as though this saved my business before it even got started.

Me, Carol Walker, Mike Warner, and my wife

A New Feeling

I THOUGHT I WAS A MAN WHEN I MET THE GENTLEMAN IN THE ELEVATOR WHO MADE A DEROGATORY REMARK ABOUT MY WIFE AND, TO HIS SURPRISE, HE FOUND HIMSELF PINNED AGAINST TWO WALLS. But starting my own business, for the first time, I *felt* like a man—I could control my own destination. I took advantage of every opportunity that came my way. Now, I was the boss. And now I had someone to boss. I allowed my position as a boss to take over all my emotions and feelings. I grew a little day by day, and things were changing. I now made the decisions that would affect not only me but also my employees and their families.

By this time, things were going well. Then I got a call from the secretary to come to Mr. Warner's office. Once I reached his office, he said, "We are going out of business."

I had been so busy trying to be a boss that I was not running my business. In my mind, all you had to do was start a business to stay in business, and the work would just come to you. I didn't know what it takes to stay in business.

And now, I was out. The plant was shutting down, and I had nowhere to go. Because of my lack of knowledge, I was stuck. At that point, I had not accumulated very much money, and the money was leaving fast.

I started searching for government projects. There were always talks about meetings for minorities in Paducah, Kentucky. I'd heard that because I was Black and had done some time in the building industry, everything would be handed to me. I got the schedule and planned to attend.

Early on the morning of the meeting, I could not sleep. I got out of bed around 4 a.m. Standing in my robe looking out my window, I noticed a robin sitting on my mailbox. He would fly down in the yard, pick around the yard with no success, and then fly back to the mailbox. Again and again, he had no luck, flying back to the mailbox. He repeated this two or three more times. Then he flew off. I thought no more about it.

The meeting was around 8 a.m. While approaching the hotel in Paducah, I turned down a side street. To my surprise, the streets were covered with earthworms on the ground. I had never witnessed this in my entire life. Immediately, I thought about the robin on the mailbox. If he flew this way, he would have all the earthworms he could eat. That is when I realized I had been sitting too long; I needed to move.

After returning home from the meeting, I realized I needed to visit more plants. But it was tough; I only had three men. Yet I had to do what I needed to do. I had a family to feed and bills to pay, as well as my employees.

I got an opportunity to bid on a project with an electrical company. I was not very experienced in quoting projects. I turned in my quote. It was going to be an open bid, and all contractors were welcome. I was the only one to show up. A young White gentleman opened the quotes at 10 a.m. After opening the quotes, he immediately stood up and closed the door. He said, "There's no one here, so change your bid."

I said, "No."

He said, "You are going to lose your butt, son." My bid was too low.

"This is my bid."

He showed me the other quotes. There was one for $48,000, another for $37,000, and mine for $5,600. I had to live with my low bid. So my company, L&C Fabrication, took the job. First, I had the challenge of finding an electrical contractor willing to collaborate with a Black contractor. Finally, a White gentleman and his son agreed to collaborate with me. I realized the robin in my yard relied on God, and L&C had to rely on man. Although I believed in God, I had to deal with the devil, which was man.

Okay, it was time to face the next challenge. What was I doing differently to make us so much cheaper? I asked the gentleman who opened the bids. He explained that the difference was the equipment and the number of men. It was time for me to sharpen my axe. Where they were using cranes, I would use a come-along and chain-falls for lifting and pulling. This could save me $12,000. The remaining cost was for the supervision, tool rental, trucks, and workforce. I saw no problem completing this project (I was going to use no equipment).

I met with the project engineer the following day to review the project with the electrician. He introduced himself as the project engineer and stated that everything would meet with his approval, bottom line. Looking directly at me, he said, "Do you understand?"

Of course, my reply was yes.

Then he explained where he wanted me to install the pipes and electrical. Then he stated that he wanted the electrical put in first. I quickly said, "This will be in the way of me running my pipe." The electrician agreed.

The engineer quickly responded, "Do you not remember my first conversation?"

I replied, "I do," while looking him in the eyes.

"I want to know how you will get these pumps in the building. And, in case you don't know, don't tear up anything in here, nor leave no mess around."

At this point, I was done talking with these engineers. The very next day, I proceeded as planned. Everything was going better than I expected. According to my quote, we were going to make at least a thousand dollars profit. All piping installed by the state code was completed.

It was time for the inspection with the engineer. He said, "First thing, I want you to move all the piping to the other side of the wall. Then, I want you to use distinct kinds of support. When you get this done, you can call me back."

"I need a change order," I replied.

"For what?" he replied. "I can change anything when and how I want. And keep in mind, you don't get paid until this passes inspection. Have a good day."

The electrician's work had passed. Mr. Walker, the electrician, looked in my direction and walked away.

What was going to be profitable was now a liability.

We finished the job and made just enough to pay my men but not the taxes.

It was time to bid on another project, which I did. Once again, I was a low-bidder. But this time, I was within $5,000. This project was 30 miles farther from the last one. I took my time and installed the work by myself. The base for this project was complete. I even thought far enough ahead to cover the unknowns. I was impressed with my bid. I was 100 percent sure we would make money this time around. I was excited going into this project.

As expected, everything went well and according to plan. I checked and double-checked—what a job! I made 100 percent sure all codes and regulations according to state code were completed. All welds were clean, the code for supports was 10 feet maximum, and I placed them nine feet apart. This was my specialty. While running projects in the building trade, companies would give the company projects only if Lawrence Butler ran the project. There was no question that I knew my stuff.

On inspection day, I couldn't wait to see his face. I was prepared and ready. The inspector walked in; he looked directly at me, and I smiled. He pulled out his pad and walked around, looking the project over. He may as well be Stevie Wonder because this was a perfect job if there ever was one.

Finally, he returned. "Everything is okay, but I want more supports before I pass this project." I replied that the state in which I held my license, which was Kentucky, where we both stood, said I was correct according to the law with this pipe insulation.

"I thought I had made myself clear on the first project, but you don't hear good, or you just don't understand. So, let's try this again. I want the hangers five feet apart; is this understood?" he said with attitude.

"You can go to hell; is that understood? You or someone like you can change it," I said. I immediately loaded my truck and went downtown to his office. I knocked on the door and asked for a meeting with the engineer's boss, which he granted.

After a short meeting, his boss said, "I'm not discrediting your word, but I have always believed in Tim and his abilities to perform his duties. Tim has been with this company for 20-plus years, and this is the first I have heard of such. Tim warned me that it may be a problem with the upcoming project because you have a tough time doing what he asks."

Seeing that I was wasting my time, I stood up and said, "You said Tim has serviced your company for 20-plus years and no problems. So, how many look like him, and how many look like me? Thanks for your time."

Donnie, the gentleman who received the bids, asked if he could say something on behalf of L&C Fabrication. He said, "There was a bid opening, and Mr. Butler was the only contractor present. I offered him an opportunity to redo his quote, but he refused to do so. For whatever it's worth, I have the utmost respect for him."

His boss said, "I hope you realize what you just said. We'll deal with that later." He stood up and exited the room.

Knowing that things were about to take another turn, I stepped out of their office. Once again, I shut my mouth; I did not want any problem with Donnie, and his boss was in the room.

James Phillips

Bill Corbitt

Butch Pierce

Martin Lagrange

A Father Figure (A Black Man)

I PAID A VISIT TO MR. HAWKINS, A BLACK GENTLEMAN I HAD ONCE RENTED FROM. I explained what was going on in my world. He asked about my business, so I explained what had been going on. He followed up with, "Do you have any work?"

"No, sir, and I guess I will never have unless I keep dealing with backward people."

He said he thought that the Black gentleman who collaborated with him had the authority to give me work. He suggested that we get in his car and visit some of his co-workers. We did, and there they put their heads together and gave what they thought was a sure way of getting me work. One was a Black female, and the other three were Black males. I left feeling great. I knew that right could only follow right, and you cannot go right and follow wrong. Now I *knew* that no matter what you do, if you are right, you will come out great.

I could not wait to collaborate with these Black people who had positioned themselves to help their own people. I got up the following day,

Mr. Hawkins

making calls and setting up a meeting. I felt so good knowing I would get the opportunity to sit with successful Black people—I knew that they were intelligent people and had had to endure to get there, though I hoped not the things I'd had to endure.

First, I met with the two gentlemen. "I'd like to help you, man, but my hands as a supervisor are tied. But I can do *this* for you; I can tell you who to contact and tell them I sent you." Same story with both Black men. And the same results, nothing but a bunch of lies.

Mr. Hawkins and his friend sent me to the other three. Then, I met with the Black woman. She entered her office and was genuinely concerned. She showed me what she could do to help and asked me about my journey to get there. It was a whole different conversation. I immediately knew the two Black guys were lying. They had the ability to give me an opportunity to work on their site, and they just weren't doing it. Not like her. Not only did I leave feeling great, but I also exited her office with some jobs, with the understanding that I had to do excellent work. And to this day, 30 years later, I am still doing jobs for her company.

During that year, I was able to obtain other small projects as well. I got up one morning and, for no reason, totally out of my norm, I decided to go through the newspaper. And to my surprise, the front page said that Custom Resins, my former employer, had a new buyer and would be re-opening soon. I approached the Custom Resins's office immediately. I saw the same secretary and asked if Mr. Warner was still there, and she said yes. She went to his office and returned, saying, "Mike said to come in." With a great big smile, I asked how he was doing. Then, I asked if it was possible for me to return to the plant and work there. "Absolutely," he said. "And Lawrence, the shop next door is available, and you can set up there."

I wasn't sure I'd heard him correctly. "I'm sorry, can you repeat that?" I asked.

And he did! "You can move into the shop and work from there."

I stood up, he stood up, and I shook his hand. As I left his office, sitting in the lobby was the gentleman who had worked in that shop before it had closed. I'd gotten there just in time; Mr. Warner had already awarded me the shop.

Two days later, to my surprise, Bill, the electrician who'd helped me on the other project, just happened to come by. He immediately recognized me. "Lawrence Butler, right?"

"Yes, sir."

"What are you doing here?" he asked.

"I started looking for work."

He mentioned the project that we'd worked on together. "I knew that guy had a problem with Black people, which I can't stand, but I stayed out of it. But anyway, have you been keeping busy?"

"No, it's been hard to get an opportunity in any of these plants. Are you looking for work?" I asked.

"We've been busy, but we can use a little more work. Do you know anyone here?"

I said yes and took him to Mr. Warner's office. After a brief introduction, I left him with Mr. Warner. After a brief meeting, he left with a project.

Before leaving, he said, "So, you've been having trouble getting into different plants?"

"Yes, I have."

"Have you tried Gibbs Die Cast?" I didn't want to say yes, and they would not return my calls. He said he would take me over and introduce me to the right guy because I was getting the runaround.

He asked who I'd been trying to talk with, and I just said, "I don't know." I didn't want to risk that his contact could be *my* contact … the contact ignoring me.

"Do you have a minute now?" he asked. I said sure. We got into his van to drive over. "I'm going to introduce you to Vaun Warner."

That very instant, I knew it was the same guy; I kept quiet. We pulled up, and there stood Vaun Warner.

The electrician greeted Vaun Warner and introduced me. "The reason I'm here is that I did a project with this young man, and he needs more work."

"Well, hell, say no more." He turned to me and said, "Hello. You should have called and asked for me," knowing that I'd been calling him for months. "Anyway," he said, "can you have six people here Monday morning?"

"Sure," I replied.

Things were taking off. Custom Resins was giving me increased projects. I was now hiring two, sometimes three, people a day. I was now a real businessperson.

My company was beginning to grow, and I didn't realize who I was becoming as it grew. I spoke to my employees as if they were nothing. I fired people for small things like being one minute late. I allowed what I thought was power to take over and control me. I became like my past bosses. I didn't like them; I hated working for them in the past.

I was the boss; I knew who I wanted to hire, and it was no one's business. I wasn't thinking Black or White; I gave everyone a chance, regardless of their color. But for some reason, a lot of Blacks were upset when I kept a White man and fired a Black man. And some of the plants had a problem with it when I brought in too many Blacks and few Whites. I fired and hired who I wanted; that was my attitude: if my guys don't like what I do, they can go somewhere else. I didn't care about their feelings or thoughts. I was the boss now. No one else mattered.

I am a big believer in being at work on time. You had to be on time. I fired my oldest and youngest

Vaun Warner

daughters for being late. So, I asked my wife if she would come and help me in the office. Her reply was, "No, you have a revolving door. I can't work for you."

I received a phone call from Mr. Hawkins. He made it clear that I was bringing all my past feelings and emotions to the present and that he was looking out for me. He knew I respected him and looked to him as a wise gentleman.

At one time, he owned a cleaning business and knew how important it was to keep employees—and how important it was how you treated them. We decided to meet for breakfast the following day.

We had breakfast the next morning as we had planned. Taking our seats, we ordered our meals, and soon, our table was filled with an array of breakfast food. The moment arrived to express gratitude for the food, and I took it upon myself to offer a heartfelt blessing.

"I thank You for this meal," I began. "May it keep us humble and bring to mind the virtues we sometimes let slip away—kindness, wisdom, love, and above all, caring and sharing. May it guide us away from our own obstacles so that we can truly reflect the virtues we aspire to. Amen."

I knew something was about to happen.

"Butler, you are incredibly wise with common sense. It's like you've been here before, an old soul. But now, you're like a train hurtling toward a crash with no survivors. You speak of your past often, but it's time to be present. You've made it through life one day at a time, and now it's time for you to be *you*. If you're a lion, you don't need to roar and mark your territory everywhere you go. People will recognize you for who you are."

Continuing, he said, "Being a business owner means challenges will find you automatically. Be prepared to face jealousy, discrimination, haters, envy, beggars, and liars—sometimes from unexpected places like family and friends. It could come from any group of people: Black, White, rich, poor, Hispanic, the churches. Direct your energy where it's most needed. You're a special cat, so be that cat going forward."

Reflecting on past management decisions, I acknowledged, "I realize now I could've had home run hitters if only I had given them more patience. I never gave the young Black ladies a chance because I saw that they didn't 'belong.' Life is often about your perceptions of someone, not who the person actually is. Now I understand you must allow yourself to know the person before you bring in your perception. Mr. Hawkins, do I really have to watch every move in the office to make sure no one steals? Can I trust my office people?"

His response to me was, "If you want to make $100 a day and the guy next to you is pocketing $50 a week, don't worry about the man stealing. You're still getting what you want, and God will take care of the rest."

At that moment, it dawned on me that my perception of being a business owner was skewed. I needed to understand that I was nothing without my team—they were the company. Though I was their boss, respect needed to flow in both directions. I was merely a director, and it hit me: I needed to appreciate them. The changes in my behavior and the person I was striving to become were not aligning with who I needed to be.

After breakfast, I headed to work. As I gathered my thoughts, the realization of how vital it was to appreciate my guys struck me. A good leader takes the team along, not leaving them behind. If you're making money, they should be right there with you. That's what a good leader does.

V&D

It occurred to me that they should have the same opportunities as me, but their actions were up to them. And that is when I made a distinction between my company and my employees.

Praising God

Looking back, I have been blessed in a way that no one could ever imagine. I have been given the opportunity to meet a family I never knew I had—I met my brothers and sisters at 19 years old, all through a basketball game. What was the chance of this ever happening?

One night, gazing at my little girl, I found renewed inspiration to reflect on my life as a ball player. It all started when I lost my "make-believe" parents—basketball. Thinking back to my 10th-grade year, I walked away from my team, my coach, and fellow players. I decided to take part in a class tournament, facing off against freshmen, juniors, and seniors—opponents we weren't expected to defeat, but we did. At that moment, I understood that Coach Leggett was handing me the recipe for life. It dawned on me for the first time that he was a remarkable man and coach.

Coach Leggett had never treated his players or students differently based on color. He consistently exhibited respectful kindness, doing everything he could for each one of us. This revelation became apparent to me as I entered the building trades. Coach Leggett was coaching Black players for the first time, and what I witnessed with him was unlike anything anyone else saw.

Coach Leggett, you provided me with the recipe for life when you taught me the essence of playing point guard, and for that, I am truly grateful! Now, I wish to share with others the invaluable lessons you imparted to me—not just to become an exceptional point guard but to evolve into a good and productive citizen within the community.

You walk like a lion but don't eat the same food. A lion roars; you can hear him six miles away. It's my time to roar, but in a different way.

All my life, I wanted brothers and sisters; I always felt alone, always crying out from inside. I went to Louisville, Kentucky, for one week. I joined a pick-up game defending a young man on the court. He was impressed with my game. He asked where I was from. When I told him, he stated that his mother was from there.

It ended up that we were related.… I went home with him to meet my father's sister for the first time. He was my cousin. One year later, I met three brothers and three sisters, along with my father.

When I look back, I can see the memories of my past that got me this far, the lessons that I've learned, and the things that I've been told. I'll never forget the story my aunt told me when I was 50 years old about when I was three or four. I had three pennies to my name and she had no clue where I had gotten them. I gave them to her because she was leaving.

Her siblings didn't like the fact that I help people. So, she told them I was giving before I knew what it was to give. Then she told me about the three pennies. That's the Lord working in me.

As a child, I was generous, but over time, I forgot where I came from. It was time to break away from the status quo and step into a leadership role. I needed to recognize that God had already provided everything I required. Equipped with the right tools, I knew I had to face challenges with the right attitude, keeping the equipment God gave me intact.

Following the blueprint for life, the Bible, was crucial. Success awaited me, a test that could be aced by facing adversity with love, just as Jesus did. The formula wasn't complicated; it was my ego and concern for others' opinions that got in the way. My past life was still very much alive, and I couldn't seem to put it to bed. It was time to look back one last time, clearing my conscience to embrace who I was meant to be—the little boy pondering the man he would become.

It became clear that carrying the burdens that were supposed to weigh me down only made me stronger. I no longer shifted blame onto others but took responsibility for navigating life with care for others and their actions.

Even as a child, I fell by the wayside of the world, which bothers me. I stole things, even though I knew better. Now, with a sense of peace, I can sleep with peace of mind after more than 10 years.

The turning point occurred during a visit to a small store in Tennessee. The same lady I had stolen from as a child, Ms. Milliken, was still alive. On Christmas Eve in 1982, as I approached her, she called my name. I immediately reached into my pocket and handed her a $100 bill, along with a big smile. She hesitated, saying she couldn't accept it, but I assured her, telling her I'd owed her for over 15 years. My conscience was clear.

My wife, who had heard the story a thousand times, told Ms. Milliken what the money was for. I knew that Ms. Milliken still had the power to lock me up—over a few pecan pies and some Red Bird Vienna Sausages that were only $0.05, so I knew my debt was paid. I wished Ms. Milliken a Merry Christmas. Leaving with a laugh, I turned to my wife, who asked, "What?" I explained that this was also why I gave to the church!

I told her how I used to lie in the room while my grandfather, the treasurer, and his cousin counted the church offering. When they weren't around, I'd look for where they kept the money but never had luck. Until one day, my grandfather got a new bed. This bed had sliding doors above the head of the bed. One day, while my grandfather and his cousin were counting the money, they had me leave the room. I listened on the other side of the wall and heard the sliding doors of the bed.

Not only did I find the money, but I also found a way to the Lord because they beat the devil out of me the next day.

Money was a necessity for me, given my background of being teased for being Black, having no parents, and being treated differently. Despite whether I had money or not, my Uncle Joe always showed me love.

Aunt Eula was the eldest and would visit my grandparents. When she visited, it was like Christmas. She was beautiful, and everyone loved her. She had her own business and a pocket full of money. She didn't mind sharing what she had with everyone and treated me like I was special. She made me feel loved, and I didn't have to buy it. She knew how my mother was about me, so she made up for it. I remember her talking to the others about how I was treated simply because I wasn't liked by my mother and had no father. She said to me, "Baby, I'm just as black as you, so don't be ashamed of your color; you're a cute little Black boy." I smiled at her in response. "See?" she said, "the only thing that hurts is what you let in."

Still, from that point on, I wanted money in my pocket. I knew family would like me (or pretend to like me) if they could smell money on me. They would listen to me in order to get the money I'd worked for. After that talk with Aunt Eula, I really learned to live where I was loved, and that was visiting cousins, going to church, and making friends in school. No one at those places ever talked about me in a negative way.

It didn't take long to realize it doesn't always work out, even in those places. You could still end up upsetting someone. I recall the time my neighbor stopped talking to me because I missed a shot, which cost us a $0.05 drink. His view of money and stuff wasn't for me—I knew I needed to stay away from people like him.

It was during high school that I realized the true value of love, freely given, and that's where it should have been all along. Life may have seemed slow, but graduating from high school surrounded by love didn't cost me a penny. It was different than the kind of "love" I felt when I gave my family money to deal with me, which I should have been shown regardless.

My aunt's advice echoed in my mind—find your love and cherish it. That was my school, GHS!

My Days after High School

I NEVER COULD HAVE IMAGINED WHAT LIFE HAD IN STORE FOR ME. My next endeavor soon taught me what life was all about. I failed to realize there was always time to sit still and allow my past to catch up. I discovered life is about finding oneself and not letting others define who you should be. The determination to be true to myself rather than succumb to others' expectations became paramount. Only I could decide whether to be *me* or let others use words to dismantle me.

Reflecting on past life lessons, I quickly learned that change is constant but must come from within. I remember some of the lessons I was told as a youngster—"Sticks and stones may break your bones, but words will never hurt me." However, as I entered the construction world, that phrase lost all meaning. On the very first day of my job, I encountered one of the most potent words ever created—the n-word. While I had heard it before, there was something different about hearing it from a White man. This word is used in so many ways with Black people. Some use it to express great talent in a basketball player, some when upset with someone, some to say "I love you," and when (and only when) we have the advantage, we use it to fight. This word, with its varied connotations among Black people, took on a new dimension in the building trade.

In the construction industry, the n-word was wielded like a tree with many branches. To some of them, we Blacks will never be equal to any White man. Its real purpose, it seemed, was to shut me down, hold me back, and break my spirit—to get into my head and control my mind by programming my way of thinking. I must admit that it served its purpose for a while. Yet, just as in basketball, if you wanted to prove someone wrong and shut their mouth, it was as simple as just getting better.

I could only draw my own conclusion for why, seemingly without reason, I had to be viewed differently. Thinking of a lion in the jungle, I realized that he is feared and unwelcome when he walks in for the first time because they're afraid he will take over just because he's a lion. Similarly, I, as a man, irrespective of color, faced unwarranted fear and resistance. It wasn't a black or white lion—just a lion. No matter what they thought, I am a man. Not black or white—just a man.

To understand what time is all about and what I've accomplished in life, I sat down with the man in me, allowing my past life to catch up. Only then could I understand many things about my life.

One of the first things I learned is that by opening my life like a door to the world, my life would never take off, and I'd never be who I was meant to be. Words can be the most powerful things we'll ever face, and how we internalize them determines their impact. From day one, the n-word was introduced into my life, with a meaning that suggested I couldn't learn, that I was fundamentally different and destined for nothing. That I wasn't a human being. This was meant to destroy me, to break my spirit, to let me know that I wasn't a man. I was like an animal with no real feelings.

However, I chose to close the door on the negativity associated with that word. Admittedly, it had a strong grip on me for a while. But as I shut out others' opinions, I started to learn. I realized that not *all*, but some were uncomfortable with me, unsure of what to say. It dawned on me that if they felt strongly about this word, perhaps there was a way to find something good in it.

Inspired by the saying "turn a lemon into lemonade," I transformed the n-word into a life-learning experience. By accepting it in a positive light, I not only learned the trade but also empowered myself to help those whom I thought others hated. Surprisingly, the word became instrumental in starting my own business, supporting my family and friends, and launching a non-profit organization. I could educate and raise my children, travel the world, and help others achieve homeownership and education.

I love what you gave me—n-word. The freedom of my own business allowed me to be anywhere I needed to support not only friends and family but anyone who needed me. You've given me the ability to keep up with school and friends, to see the other side of the world that I never expected to be able to see, to put kids in school, and to meet new friends, such as the Amish.

I just finished my 50th school reunion, and because of you, I could represent. I left home; in some people's minds, we all were the n-word, but that night, we were brothers and sisters, my race with love and kindness, which drifted over to all the Whites and Blacks who, in return, handed love back to us during our 50th class reunion.

You've given me the freedom to be observed by other kids and to help change so many people who were bad. You would not believe how many Whites have come up to me and said, "Your attitude has buried that word in my heart."

Looking back, I had a choice the first time you said it to me; I could have reacted like any normal man with pride and ego. Instead, I took it by dropping my head in disrespect and shame. And if I must relive it again, I will take that word with a smile; instead of the head down and shame, the heart would be open for love. I thank all the people who used this word because it encouraged me, motivated me, and supported me to be the man that I am today.

The n-word, once a source of pain, granted me the ability to handle adversity with composure. It led to unexpected gifts, like a Mustang Roush. The word even helped me understand my coach, who had freedom yet never thought to use this word. He departed on September 3 but left me some very important recipes for life, which he had the chance to hear from me himself.

Bobbie Jarrett

Al Baity

Ellis Reed

Jeff Walker

The Quarters of Life

FIRST QUARTER

THE FIRST QUARTER OF LIFE IS YOUR BABY YEARS. These are supposedly the happiest years of your life; you are alive and a living gift to help beautify the earth. This is God's plan. You are given two coaches who work together as one—your mother and father. Through them, you learn to love by being loved; you learn respect by giving respect; you learn discipline by being taught; you learn to forgive through forgiveness; you learn to share from sharing; you learn to honor thy mother and thy father by telling the truth no matter what the consequences may be.

No matter how our minds are uniquely shaped, some things are naturally built in us. We are human and can easily be influenced. We can easily lie and influence others to lie. We can easily embrace ourselves, not willing to share or care about anyone other than ourselves. This is naturally built inside of us, which is why we are handed two coaches and one rule book: the Bible. In basketball, we learn how to play the game during practice, but this is life, where your rule book teaches you various lessons.

> "Train up a child in the way that he should go, and
> they will not depart from you."
> —Proverbs 22:6 (NKJV)

There are seven rules of life:
1. Sticks and stones may break your bones, but words shall never hurt you.
2. Let it go.
3. Ignore them.
4. Don't compare.

5. Stay calm.
6. It's on you.
7. Smile.

Now it's time to go to the second quarter.

SECOND QUARTER

The second quarter is vulnerable. You get to walk out onto the floor alone for the first time, and the world is handed to you. This is your wilderness, where you can either follow your instructions, your coaches' instructions, or, as most do, your own way.

In the second quarter of a basketball game, you think you have it figured out, and that's when you realize your coaches didn't know what they're talking about. You can now do it your way; this is what we consider halftime. This is when you go into the locker room and regroup. Just like a basketball game or a football game, in the game of life, you graduate from high school and college—do you have what it takes to get back out there?

When you sit back and look at the things the world has to offer, some things can be detrimental, only because you don't really know what all is involved. As the saying goes, everything that glitters is not gold. Just like a nut, not everything inside is always good once it's cracked. It's like taking a wife without God, and it's not going to end up how it should be.

Matthew 4:9 says, "'All this I will give you,' he said, 'if you will bow down and worship me'" (NIrV). In the wilderness, Jesus was offered all the things the city possessed, and it was up to Him to choose to be faithful or not. But He was obedient. Like Him, you also have a choice. Once you look at all the city has to offer, from lying, cheating, sex, stealing, competing, jealousy, and envy, you must learn how to navigate it. You can choose to embrace it or live a higher purpose. Lying is so prominent now that when comparing it to playing a sport, you often need instant replay to get to the truth. If 10 people dropped the ball during the Super Bowl, how many of them would tell the truth if there were no instant replay?

Standing in that one arena for that one event, you can easily find everything the city has to offer without even stepping into the city. What you decide here will impact how you enter the third quarter of your life.

THIRD QUARTER

The third quarter of life is working God's plan to share your life with someone. Like in basketball, the third quarter of life is about getting serious, living from your purpose, and life partnerships. For many, this comes with a career, starting a family, and owning a home. The most beautiful thing that one can find in this quarter is a God-chosen husband or wife. This quarter is when you are serious about life and retirement. You want the best for retirement, so you start saving the 401K, the Roth IRA, the SIMPLE IRA plan.

You have to be careful in this quarter of life. This is where you can lose focus on your purpose and get caught up in what the person beside you has. Money can mess with your happiness. You can shower your kids with everything they desire, but at the same time, it can be a tool to hold people back. You start using it to push your agenda, turn lies into truths, and position yourself to manipulate and mistreat others. It's like this power trip where you can boast and brag about your success, but deep down, you know it's not all on the up-and-up.

You start using what you've got from the system and your appearance to boost yourself and your crew, all under the guise of calling it success. And you're fully aware that you got it unfairly. It messes with your head, making you believe you can keep the next person down like you have some control. It's a twisted game that money plays on your values and principles.

First Timothy 6:10 says, "For the love of money is the root of all evil: which while some coveted after, they have erred from the faith, and pierced themselves through with many sorrows."

Obedience to God will allow you to have the things that are not only good for you but right for you. "With man this is impossible, but with God all things are possible" (Matt. 19:26).

The degree to which you get lost in the "stuff" of this world will determine how you close out your final quarter. So don't let stuff pull you in the wrong direction.

FOURTH QUARTER

In the fourth quarter of life, you're at the scoreboard, and it shows either "faithful" or "unfaithful." This is the quarter where you get the instant replay of your entire life.

I recall walking into the courtroom with my daughter, surrounded by the superintendent and principal; my daughter was involved in the unfair treatment of Black kids and got called the n-word. So, she stood up for Black kids, including herself, for discrimination against the school system by coaches, teachers, so-called friends, students, preachers, parents, and even a member of the NAACP—all lying to prevent a child from living a normal life. Leaving the courtroom that day, I never thought the truth of that incident would see the light outside those walls, let alone that I'd end up writing a book.

This book isn't just for me; it's for everyone around me. We all get a shot at starting over in the fourth quarter of our lives, but forgiveness has to come first. And it started with me.

Believe it or not, that day, I asked God to forgive them for all the lies told in that courtroom. My mind had accepted it, but my heart took a while, until today. Luke 12:48 hit me—"But he that knew not, and did commit things worthy of stripes, shall be beaten with few stripes. For unto whomsoever much is given, of him shall be much required: and to whom men have committed much, of him they will ask the more" (KJV).

I had the means to stand up and slow down how African American kids were being treated, which many before me probably didn't. In the moment, it felt like I had lost, and the courtroom probably felt victorious. But then it hit me—just like turning something sour into something sweet, what if I squeeze the courtroom and see what comes out today?

There was a lady who stood up for what was right and lost her job of nine years. It turned out to be a blessing. She ended up with a better job with better benefits. A gentleman stood up for what was right in that courtroom and lost his job—but now he's making three times more in a new job. Another lady from that courtroom went on to do more than anyone thought possible in Henderson, Kentucky. Another young lady from that day came in from the Pentagon and lives an amazing life today. Another young lady who had the heart to stand up against the entire system is a dental surgeon today.

One gentleman was told that if he didn't drop the lawsuit, he would never work in that plant again, and he was let go. Today, he's the owner of not one, not two or three, but *four* companies.

Back then, it felt like God had forgotten it all, but now I see it differently, thinking of 1 John 4:4—"You, dear children, are from God and have overcome them because the one who is in you is greater than the one who is in the world."

Tears of hurt and shame turned into tears of joy.

It all boils down to your retirement. The things you achieve in this world, if you're part of the world, stay here when you leave. That's the world's retirement, and it ends when you do. But if He is in you, your retirement plan starts when you leave this world, and it's eternal life. Your book is open with your name on it, and forgiveness is the only thing standing between the two books. So, where do you stand?

Stuff	**You?**	**Eternal Life**
World's Retirement	Forgiveness	God's Retirement

Linsey Butch-Banker

Mary Ligon

Acknowledgments

Many people have made my life what it is today. And while I can't name all of them, I would like to acknowledge the following people:

- Pastor Robert A. Esters: He tutored me which enabled me to gain apprenticeship in plumbing.
- Bill Hastie
- Bruce Pullem
- Grandparents
- Mary Ligon
- Ray Butler
- Linsey Butch-Banker
- Uncle Joe
- Aunt Juanita Range
- Principal Lathem
- Elizabeth
- Aunt Eula
- Classmates
- Parents
- All friends and family
- Mike Warner
- James E. Phillips
- Bill Corbitt
- Martin Lagrange
- Jeffrey Cruse
- Mary Thompson
- Butch Pierce
- Steve Sitzmen
- Al Baity

- Vaun Warner
- Jeff Walker
- Ellis Redd
- V&D
- Founders – Nick & Fannie Graber
- Gerald L. Diener
- Lonnie Eicher
- Barbara M. Graber
- Elmer L. Graber
- Floyd R. Graber
- Jalon M. Graber
- Japheth F. Graber
- John D. Graber
- Jonas D. Graber
- Kenneth J. Graber
- Lori Graber
- Marvin Graber
- Marvin R. Graber
- Matthew J. Graber
- Menno Graber
- Nicholas H. Graber
- Phillip R. Graber
- Samuel J. Graber
- Sharon R. Graber
- Justin Knepp
- Phillip Knepp
- Stanley Knepp
- Nicholas R. McCarter
- Beau A. Pierce
- Freeman Raber
- Jonas A. Raber
- Matthew Raber
- Nicholas A. Raber

- Vernon A. Raber
- Robert L. Schwartz
- Paul J. Stoll
- Stephen Stoll
- John Swartzentruber
- Barbara Wagler
- Chad Wagler
- Dreyton Wagler
- Henry J. Wagler
- Lavern M. Wagler
- Leon M. Wagler
- Malinda Wagler
- Marvin S. Wagler
- Matthew Wagler
- Olen Wagler
- Rebecca Wagler
- John Weaver

Dear Friends

I hope you enjoyed *Untamed*. If you were inspired by the book, we invite you to ask your friends and relatives to read it as well.

Here are a few ways that you can help us spread the word:

- Recommend the book to friends – word-of-mouth is still the most effective form of advertising.
- Purchase additional copies to give away as gifts on my website.
- Post a 5-Star review on Amazon.
- Write about the book on your Facebook, X, Instagram, LinkedIn—any social media you use!
- If you blog, consider referencing the book, or publishing an excerpt from the book with a link back to my website. You have my permission to do this if you provide proper credit and backlinks.

The best way to connect is by visiting
BookOfLoveHateAndJealousy.com.

www.ingramcontent.com/pod-product-compliance
Lightning Source LLC
Chambersburg PA
CBHW050033040726
47599CB00015B/1663